THE SEVEN CITIES OF DELHI

DIWĀN KHĀS IN THE PALACE.

[*Frontispiece.*

THE SEVEN CITIES OF DELHI

By

GORDON RISLEY HEARN

GYAN

Published by

Gyan Publishing House
5, Ansari Road
Daryaganj, New Delhi-110002
Phone: 011-47034999, 9811692060
E-mail: books@gyanbooks.com

Distribution Network
gyanbooks.com
India, USA, Canada, UK, Australia, France

ISBN : 978-81-212-6617-8 (PB)
First Published, 1906

2nd Impression 2022

Printed at: Gyan Press, Delhi.

THE SEVEN CITIES OF DELHI
Author: Gordon Risley Hearn

THE SEVEN CITIES OF DELHI

BY

GORDON RISLEY HEARN

CAPTAIN, ROYAL ENGINEERS

ASSOCIATE OF THE INSTITUTION OF CIVIL ENGINEERS

1906

PREFACE

THE arrangement of this book is the result of much consideration and of more than one alteration. As it stands, the book is divided into three parts. In the first, the situations of the seven cities, and of the principal monuments, are given. The second part treats of archæology and architecture. The third part gives the history of Delhi from the Mahomedan conquest to the present time.

This arrangement increases the utility of the work to those who wish to use it as a guide-book also. The two chapters of the first part have been written in the form of itineraries for two days, the time which experience has shown is usually devoted to Delhi by the majority of travellers. Actual tests have shown that what has been written is not too much for the time allotted, and leaves time to notice details, which can be looked up in the second part. The names in black type are sufficient indication to the guide or coachman where next to proceed, and the itineraries follow the usual routes, which my experience of the lighting of the subjects has shown to be the best. For instance, the Ridge is best seen in the afternoon.

In the second part the monuments have been grouped by cities, and four more days can usefully be spent in examining them. The history in the third part will be much better appreciated by those who have followed the itineraries (even if only on the map), and the visitor can read it at leisure. The Siege of 1857 has received its due share of attention, and every single scene of those stirring events has been pointed out.

It will be noticed that the *a* is sometimes accented. Ordinarily it should be pronounced as the *u* in sum; thus Akbar is pronounced Uckbur; but *ā* is pronounced as in the word father. For the names of places the Indian Postal Guide has been followed; this publication retains the old spelling for the well-known places.

Nearly all the photographs have been specially taken by myself; I have also prepared the maps. A magnifying glass will show up many of the finer details if the plates are held in a strong light. The view of the Kutb Minār should be held above the level of the eyes; this corrects the leaning back, which is otherwise apparent in photographs of high buildings.

Preface

A list of the works consulted will be found in the Appendix. The libraries of the British Museum, India Office, and East India United Service Club have all been searched for information. Great care has been taken to get this correct, but many instances could be given where accounts differ, especially in the dates. I shall always be grateful for further information.

To the following gentlemen I am specially indebted for kindly giving me their personal experiences :—

Sir Alexander Taylor, G.C.B., explained the making of the Custom-house Battery. Mr. T. Gateley, late Bengal Horse Artillery, and Rāi Bahādur Janki Nāth, showed me the scenes of the Siege. Mr. J. S. Aldwell related the story of the defence of a house in Dariāganj, and pointed out the sites of several buildings now destroyed. Shaikh Sharf-ud-din, guardian of the shrine of Nizām-ud-din, pointed out the points of interest in that vicinity. Badri Dās, a guide of fifty years' standing, took me round the old cities.

I would add my thanks to several Government officials for their courtesy.

G. R. H.

LONDON,
November, 1906.

CONTENTS

SITUATIONS OF THE OBJECTS OF INTEREST (ITINERARIES FOR TWO DAYS)

CHAPTER I

MODERN DELHI AND THE RIDGE

CHAPTER II

THE PLAINS TO THE SOUTH OF DELHI

Contents

DETAILED DESCRIPTIONS OF THE CITIES AND THEIR MONUMENTS

CHAPTER III

THE SEVEN CITIES OF DELHI

CHAPTER IV

OLD DELHI

CHAPTER V

SIRI, TUGHLUKĀBĀD, AND JAHĀNPANĀH

Contents

CHAPTER VI

FIROZĀBĀD AND THE DELHI OF SHER SHĀH

CHAPTER VII

SHĀHJAHĀNĀBĀD

HISTORY OF DELHI FROM THE TWELFTH TO THE TWENTIETH CENTURIES

CHAPTER VIII

DELHI BEFORE THE MOGHAL CONQUEST

Contents

CHAPTER IX

DELHI IN MOGHAL TIMES

CHAPTER X

DELHI UNDER "JOHN COMPANY"

CHAPTER XI

THE MUTINY OF 1857 AND THE SIEGE

CHAPTER XII

DELHI SINCE 1857

LIST OF ILLUSTRATIONS

List of Illustrations

PLANS

THE SEVEN CITIES OF DELHI

CHAPTER I

MODERN DELHI AND THE RIDGE

The Indian Rome—The modern city—Cashmere Gate—St. James's Church—Magazine—The Fort—Palace buildings—Delhi Gate—Jāma Masjid—Chāndni Chouk—Queen's Gardens—Mori Gate—The Ridge—Mound piquet—Old cantonments—Military cemetery—Flagstaff Tower—Hindu Rāo's house—Siege batteries—Kudsia Gardens—Custom-house battery—Cashmere Bastion.

Map of Delhi in 1857, *p.* 172.
Map of the Siege-Works, p. 294.

DELHI has well been described as the Indian Rome. It has been the imperial city of India for over seven hundred years, and the seven hills of Rome are represented by the seven cities of Delhi. In modern Rome the hills are difficult to distinguish, because of the many buildings, which cover the whole site; modern Delhi only occupies a small portion of the sixty square miles, over which are scattered the monuments of its former greatness, and the abandoned cities are difficult to distinguish on the deserted plains.

Before we proceed to examine the monuments in any detail, or to recount the history attached to them, it is desirable that the reader should be well acquainted with their situation. The most convenient way to ensure this is to follow itineraries, which will conduct him within sight of all the important monuments; the principal features of these will be noticed, so as to fix their significance in the mind. It should be understood that, in unfolding the panoramas, we shall follow the direction taken by the hands of a clock—that is, from left to right. The position of the various buildings is given left or right of the direction in which the road is leading.

Modern Delhi is still contained within the walls of Shāhjahānābād, the last of the seven cities, and built by the third great Moghal emperor, whose name is so well known as the builder of that magnificent mausoleum at Agra, commonly known as the "Tāj Mahāl," and the admiration of the world. The walls, starting from the Water Bastion on the north face, run practically west for five-sixths of a mile to the Mori Bastion, and thence curve in a great arc, of a length of nearly three miles, to the river at the Wellesley Bastion; they then follow the river-bank to the Water

Bastion again, their line broken by the "Fort," which lies about midway in this last face. The principal street is the famous Chāndni Chouk, running east and west from the Lahore Gate of the Castle to the Lahore Gate of the city, with a slight detour at the Fatehpuri Masjid. This street may be said to divide the native quarter from the commercial portion, which includes the railway-station yards, into which no fewer than seven lines of railway now run.

The special objects of interest are the Castle, now called the "Fort," which contains the palace; the Jāma Masjid, which is the finest mosque in all India; and many a building of interest in connection with the Mutiny and with the massacre which followed the arrival of the rebels from Meerut, on May 11, 1857.

Cashmere Gate.—The city is entered from the "Civil Lines" by the Cashmere Gate, which, originally a single gateway, was rebuilt and enlarged by one of the Bengal Engineers, Major Robert Smith. It was here that a famous act of bravery—the blowing in of the gateway during the assault in September, 1857—was performed; a tablet, erected by Lord Napier of Magdala, records some of the names of those who took part in the desperate deed. Inside this gate, there was, in 1857, an enclosure, surrounded by a case-mated wall, part of which still abuts on the ramparts; in this the main guard mounted, the officer having his quarters over what is now the police-station. It was thus necessary to pass the guard in order to enter the city. A door on the left of the enclosure gave access to the courts and treasury.

St. James's Church (p. 136).—The Church of St. James is near by, and contains many a record of foul murder done, not unavenged. Two tablets to the memory of the families of Mr. Beresford (Manager of the Delhi Bank) and of a Mr. Collins, numbering together twenty-five persons, show how thoroughly the rebels, assisted by the scum of the city, destroyed every Christian they could find. It is pleasant to be able to record that there were merciful men in Delhi, and that one woman was sheltered up to the 19th of August, on which date she was aided to escape to the British camp.

In the churchyard are the ball and cross, which formerly adorned the top of the dome; they were shot at by the mutineers in the hope that by their fall might be ensured the expulsion of the English. Here, also, is the vault of the family of Colonel James Skinner, C.B., who was at one time in the employ of the Mahārāja Scindia of Gwalior, but left him when he went to war with the English; he afterwards entered the Company's service, and raised a regiment of irregular horse, known by his name to this day. He built this church in fulfilment of a vow, made while lying wounded on a battlefield. Some say that he also vowed to build a mosque and a temple, pointing out, as erected by him, a pretty little mosque close to his house, the upper story of which shows above the roofs of the shops bordering the road. But this is not so, for the mosque, called Fakhr-ul-Masājid, though doubtless used by the Musulmāni ladies of his family for worship, was built in 1728, before his time.

Opposite the church is a triangular plot of land, now enclosed, on the other side of which is a road. This, before the railway cut it off, led direct to the Chāndni Chouk, and was followed by one of the columns after the assault in 1857; but the enemy mustered too strong, and drove the column back again to this neighbourhood.

Magazine (p. 138).—The road to the palace passes between the modern St. Stephen's College and a hostel attached to it (both in charge of the Cambridge Mission), and then runs between some shops and past the Government College (once the Residency) to the "Magazine," or Arsenal, now occupied by the telegraph and post offices. In 1857 the telegraph-office was near the Ridge, and a granite obelisk, erected outside the present one, records the pluck of two signallers, mere lads, who sent to Umballa messages, which gave warning and "saved the Punjab." The post-office is in the old armoury, and close by still stands a powder-magazine. The main gateway is nearly all that remains of the surrounding walls; over the gate is a tablet recording the names of nine resolute men, who defended the arsenal as long as they could, and eventually blew up part of it in the face of the enemy.

Cemetery (p. 140).—Next to the arsenal is an old cemetery, abandoned in 1855 for one outside the Cashmere Gate.

Canal.—Having passed under the Lothian railway-bridge, the road ascends a slope, the old river-bank. At the top is a bridge over a small canal; this, entering near the Cabul Gate, irrigates the Queen's Gardens. The water used to flow into the castle gardens, and ripple through the apartments of the palace; it also drove some mills, now demolished, near the Nigambodh Gate. To the right, on now open ground, which was cleared after 1857, used to be the post-office, and on the left was Major Abbott's house—now the Volunteer armoury. The Delhi Bank lies among trees to the right.

The old road runs to the left from the small bridge over the canal; near the castle walls, it crosses the old Grand Trunk Road, which, entering the city by the Calcutta Gate, passed the garden of Mādho Dās (p. 142), traversed the Chāndni Chouk, and emerged from the city by the Lahore Gate. The Calcutta Gate, built in 1852, has been removed to admit the railway, and this portion of the Trunk Road has been abandoned. An avenue of trees, parallel to the castle walls, still marks the line of an old road to Dariāganj, and to the Rājghāt Gate, opposite which a bridge of boats used to lie, up to the year 1852; after that year it was moved to opposite the Calcutta Gate. Formerly there was a large tank, named after Lord Ellenborough, just above this road, and near the corner of the fort; this was filled from a branch of the canal which flowed through the Chāndni Chouk. The channel has now been covered over and the water shut off, and the tank has been filled in.

The Fort (p. 142).—The castle, with its rose-red sandstone walls, is entered by the Lahore Gate, over which are rooms, occupied in May, 1857, by the Captain of the Palace Guard.

Here were done to death the captain, the commissioner, the magistrate, the chaplain, his daughter, and a young lady friend; also a man unknown, who is said to have been a portrait-painter. Beyond the portal is a fine vaulted passage, with rooms on either side, meant, no doubt, for the guard in Moghal times. Facing the exit from this passage is the Nakkār-Khāna, or music-gallery, in which a museum has been recently formed. Under a large tree, which stood on the north of the vaulted entrance, were collected, five days after the outbreak of the Mutiny, a considerable number of poor people, who had surrendered, and had been taken into the palace, on a promise that their lives should be spared. Forgetful of the proverb, "Trust a cobra, not an Afghān!" they were nearly all butchered; only a very few were spared, and told the terrible story at the king's trial.

Diwān Ām (p. 146).—The road now makes a slight detour to avoid the music-gallery, at the gate under which all nobles had to dismount from their elephants, and approach on foot, or in palanquin, the Hall of Public Audience—Diwān Ām. This noble hall is built in the Hindu style, with sixty pillars of red sandstone carrying cross-beams, and a roof of flat slabs. Once upon a time these pillars were covered with polished limewash, like those in the Public Audience Hall in the palace at Agra; but the lime has flaked off, and the building has a somewhat gloomy appearance. What a contrast to the splendid scenes of the days of Shāh Jahān and of Aurangzeb! when a magnificent tent, lined with flowered chintzes, and supported by poles "as high as the masts of a barque," was pitched between this hall and the music-gallery: when the court in front was filled by a brilliant throng of nobles; when the emperor sat on his Peacock Throne, while ambassadors from all countries brought rare gifts and paid their respects. Such a scene was sufficient to bring men thousands of miles to see the Court of the Great Moghal; one man, Tom Coryate, in the days of King James the First, walked most of the way in order to do so. Now, however, the Moghal courtiers rest in their nameless graves; the ashes of the Hindu princes have long been consigned to the Ganges or Jumna; the Peacock Throne was taken by Nādir Shāh to Persia in 1739; and the last King of Delhi died, a prisoner, in Rangoon. These buildings also would crumble into dust, were it not for the care of Government; and descendants of kings work, but not very hard, for their living.

There is a raised throne, of carved marble and

inlaid work against the back wall. In the recess behind it are some pictures in "pietra dura," recently returned from the South Kensington Museum; others, again, have been restored by the orders of Lord Curzon, who, at his own expense, imported an Italian artist from Florence to carry out the work. On a seat below the throne sat the Prime Minister, rising from time to time to present a petition to the King for his perusal.

It must not be supposed that this throne is the famous Peacock Throne, which appears to have been a sort of four-poster marble bed, movable, and covered with jewels. It was valued at Rs.107,000,000 by Tavernier, a French connoisseur, who "travelled" in works of art, and saw it in the seventeenth century. It is now in the palace of the Shah of Persia at Teherān, and has, more recently, been appraised at £2,600,000.

There are two doors to the right of the throne in the wall, the further giving access by steps to the recess behind the throne, while the nearer gave entrance to the private gardens. Formerly there was a gate in the wall of an inner court abutting on the north end of the hall; through this court the privileged entered, by a slightly devious route, the court in front of the Hall of Private Audience. The door now used led to the Imtiāz Mahal, among the part given up to the women. The gardens are now in process of restoration, but can never regain the aspect which once they must have presented, when fair ladies in many-hued dresses filled the gay scene, and the cloistered courts resounded with their laughter. At the beginning of the last century, the interior of the castle presented a mixture of tawdry show and squalor amid magnificent surroundings; the King found it rather difficult to meet expenses on his income of over thirteen lakhs of rupees (which included allowances from the Company to himself and his family), and the courtiers saw very little pay. After the Mutiny, many of the buildings were cleared away and barracks were built for the garrison, which now consists of two companies of European infantry and a company of garrison artillery.

Diwān Khās (p. 150).—The lovely Hall of Private Audience, or Diwān Khās, which alone among the private apartments was used for the reception of ministers, nobles, or ambassadors, stands on the river-wall. It is faced with marble, painted or inlaid, and, with costly awnings on all sides, and Persian carpets on the floor, must have looked splendid, and have justified the inscription above the arches at the ends of the centre room—

The Seven Cities of Delhi

"If Paradise be on the face of the earth,
It is this, even this, it is this."

Once the Peacock Throne stood in this hall; when that had been carried away a canopied throne of wood, covered with thin gold plates, was substituted. This, presumably, was broken up after the Mutiny. Another throne of block crystal, which used to stand in this hall, is now at Windsor; this may have come from Arangpur, a few miles south of Delhi. There remains now only a marble seat.

Khās Mahal (p. 156).—Next to the Diwān Khās is a little group of buildings, the "Picture Room" and "Octagon Tower" adjoining, which the king himself occupied. Projecting over the river-wall is a rather modern balcony, constructed by Akbar Shāh the Second; from this he used to show himself daily to his subjects, assembled in the river-bed below; this was an ancient custom, instituted by the Great Akbar. Many Hindus would not take their food unless they had attended this ceremony, which was considered of great importance, and rightly so, for who knew if the emperor were alive, if he did not appear? Palace intrigue was thoroughly understood in those days.

Rang Mahal (p. 158).—Next to the private apartments of the king is the "Rang Mahal," or "Painted Palace," the term "Mahal" being particularly applied to the women's apartments. This was used after 1857 as an officers' mess-room, and has been much disfigured by white-wash, but is now being restored. Underneath are rooms which were used for retreat during summer heats. Beyond this hall were other apartments for the women, and through the whole range of the buildings on the terrace flowed water in a channel.

Across this channel, in the Khās Mahal, there is an exquisite inlaid and pierced marble screen, so thin as to be translucent in the upper part, where are depicted the sun, moon, and stars, and the scales of Justice; the lower part is like lace, so delicate is the carving. A pierced marble balustrade filled in the intervals between the pillars in the Diwān Khās, but this has gone, like the precious stones of the inlay-work; some taken by the Mahrattas, with the silver plates which once formed the ceiling; some, it is to be feared, by modern vandals.

Baths (p. 152).—On the north side of the Diwān Khās is a range of baths. They consist of a cool room, looking out over the river, and two hot rooms, heated from below by furnaces. The inlaid floors and dados are very beautiful; the paintings, which formerly adorned the upper part of the walls and the roofs, have been hidden by whitewash.

Pearl Mosque.—Next to the baths is a lovely little "Pearl" Mosque, built by Aurangzeb as a private chapel for himself and the ladies of the zenāna, who could obtain entrance by a door (now closed) to the right of the covered portion. On the floor are marble slabs of a prayer-carpet pattern, showing each person where to stand, and in the centre of the open court is the usual ablutionary basin, fed by water from below. The door is of bronze, and a flight of stairs close by leads to the top of the walls, whence it is apparent that the outer sides of the walls conform to the lines of the baths and other buildings, but the inner sides are carefully oriented towards Mecca; the difference in direction is but slight, but was too important to be overlooked. The marble domes look heavy, but they have replaced domes of copper gilt, which were sold by auction for a mere song, after the siege in 1857. A similar fate befell the dome over the Octagon Tower and the small domes on the Diwān Khās, all of which were of gilded copper plates.

PEARL MOSQUE.

[To face p. 14.

To the north and south of this group of buildings, only a few scattered pavilions remain, one near the Shāh Burj at the north end of the river-terrace, three others (p. 155) close by, which stood in a garden-court, which has been demolished, and one or two more on the river-wall—sole survivors of the buildings which stretched from the Shāh Burj to the baths, and again from the Rang Mahal to the Asd Burj tower near the Water Gate, in the south-east corner of the fort. The courts, which once existed for the seclusion of the women, have all been removed.

Delhi Gate.—At the south-western corner of the fort is the Delhi Gate, on either side of which stands a stone elephant, recently restored; the riders represent Jāimal and Patta, two Rājput chiefs, killed, after a desperate struggle, in the emperor's darbār. The leaves of the gate are fitted with long spikes, placed high up, in order to resist a charge by elephants.

Golden Mosque.—Outside the Delhi Gate is a pretty little mosque, with gilded minarets; this escaped the general demolition of buildings round the fort, which followed the events of 1857. The quarter of Dariāganj lies among some trees to the south, where two tall towering minarets mark the mosque called "Zinat-ul-Masājid," the "beauty among mosques." A road to the Rājghāt Gate, now filled up, ran in between the castle and Dariāganj, and near the gilded mosque was the staging bungalow; in this two officers, whose names are unknown, met their death on the morning of the outbreak of the Mutiny.

Jāma Masjid (p. 165).—The road to the Jāma Masjid ran past elephant stables, on the left, and through a bāzār and "chouk," all of which have been swept away, thereby opening up a splendid view of the magnificent mosque, which stands on high, erected as it is on an outcrop of rock, called the Jujula Pahār. The Jāma Masjid is the cathedral mosque of India, and here on Fridays all assemble for prayer, the service on other days being attended in the parish mosques. The word "Jāma" means "collected together," and must not be confused with "Juma," which means "Friday." The efficacy of prayers at home being counted as one, to pray in the Jāma Masjid brings the reward of twenty-five prayers, while a prayer in the Kabah at Mecca is equal to one hundred thousand. During the month of Ramzān (which now falls in October, but constantly advances, for the Mahomedan year is a lunar year) an enormous congregation assembles here at 1.30 p.m. on Fridays; it is a most impressive sight to see the long lines of worshippers rising, falling, waving like corn in a hurricane. But it is still more impressive at sunset, when the Muezzins call to prayer from the minarets, after two bombs have been fired to announce the termination of the obligatory fast, and, in the gathering darkness, the murmur of prayer echoes through the gloomy domes.

In the centre of the courtyard is an ablutionary tank; the covered mosque proper, with its three bulbous domes, lies along the western side; and in one corner of the surrounding colonnades is a room, where are kept certain relics of Mahomed and of other saints. On a pillar in the court is engraved an old map of the world.

Daribā.—From the Jāma Masjid runs a street called the Daribā, through which one column tried to gain the Jāma Masjid on the day of the assault, but, being opposed by overwhelming odds, had to retire again. On either side, where this street debouches into the Chāndni Chouk, are the remains of gateposts of the "Khuni Darwāza," or "bloody gate." When Nādir Shāh, the Persian, entered Delhi in 1739, there was a scuffle between some of his men and the inhabitants, in the course of which some Persians were killed and he himself was fired at. Transported with rage, he ordered a wholesale massacre of the people, and watched it from the Golden Mosque of Roshan-ud-dāula, not far from here. The slaughter continued from eight in the morning until three in the afternoon, and over a hundred thousand are said to have perished, the streets being blocked with the dead.

Kotwāli.—Close to the Golden Mosque is the Kotwāli, or principal police-station, opposite which were exposed the bodies of three princes, whom Hodson shot, in 1857. Here also were erected gallows, on which many a rebel suffered the last penalty, under the eye (it is said) of Sir Theophilus Metcalfe, exasperated at the loss of his magnificent mansion and the many treasures which it contained.

Chāndni Chouk.—The name "Chāndni Chouk" means silver market-place, and was originally given to an octagonal court built by Jahanāra Begam, daughter of Shāhjahān. The name is now given to the street, which extends on either side. The jewellers' shops are here. A channel, in which water once flowed down the centre of the street, has long been covered over, but all down the centre are kiosks, in which

Brahmins give water to Hindus, at the expense of the charitable, while Mahomedan water-carriers clink brass dishes to summon their thirsty co-religionists.

Queen's Gardens.—In the centre of the Chouk a clock tower has been erected; opposite this is the town hall, containing a museum. In this is an interesting panoramic photograph of the city, which was taken in 1857, shortly after the recapture; it shows the streets, usually teeming with people, to be absolutely deserted. At the back of the town hall are the "Queen's Gardens," the Hyde Park of Delhi, bounded by the Queen's Road, which leads to the Dufferin Railway Bridge, and to the Cabul Gate, near which is a marble tablet, recording the spot where John Nicholson was mortally wounded. At the corner of the gardens is the house of Bahādur Jang Khān, now occupied by the Cambridge Mission, whose church is close by. Near here also, on the banks of the canal, were the palace and baths of Saādat Khan, brother of Ali Mardān Khān, who constructed the canal.

Mori Gate.—A road over the Dufferin Railway Bridge leads to a gap in the walls, once closed by the Mori Gate, which has been removed since the Mutiny, in order to give freer egress and ingress to the increased traffic. From the Mori Gate several diverging roads lead into the civil lines.

North of the city lies the famous Ridge, which was occupied by the avenging army, when it appeared before the city on the 8th of June; from it the rebels tried again and again, but all in vain, to drive the little force, unable to do more than retain their position until the arrival of Nicholson's column and the siege-train. The siege-batteries were started on the 7th of September; after one short week of trenches and two days and nights of battering, the city was assaulted and entered on the 14th of September. But the enemy were still full of fight, and it was not until the 20th of the month that the troops, exhausted with their exertions and with five days of street-fighting, were able to occupy the whole city, and to drink the Queen's health in the Diwān Khās.

On the ground around the Ridge, and up to the walls, are many interesting objects, which tell the story of this strenuous struggle by which India was saved.

Mound Piquet.—From the Cashmere Gate, past Ludlow Castle and Maiden's Hotel, runs the Alipur Road, which, at a point beyond the

Commissioner's house, dips and crosses a ravine. Here the road bifurcates, the left-hand road leading to the round red Flagstaff Tower on the Ridge. Opposite the rise of the right-hand road is a mound, which is an old brick-kiln, and was occupied by a piquet during the siege; the earthworks on the top may still be traced.

From the top of this mound an excellent panoramic view of the situation is obtained. On the left are the ruins of Metcalfe House, built, in 1844, by Sir Thomas Metcalfe, then Resident at the Court of the King of Delhi; his son was joint-magistrate at the time of the outbreak. Down the river is the red railway bridge, occupying very much the same position as the bridge of boats did in 1857; the railway was then actually under construction, on much the same alignment as that of the Agra-Delhi Chord Railway. At the near end of the bridge rise the red walls of the fort, enclosing the barracks, and the British flag may be discerned floating over the Lahore Gate. Next, and a good deal nearer, appears the yellow dome of St. James's Church, close to the Cashmere Gate. Nearer still, are the red walls of Maiden's Hotel, almost in a line with the domes and minarets of the Jāma Masjid, and the towers of the railway station show just above the trees.

Then, to the right, a peculiar building, with a square tank on the top and a chimney close by, marks the corner of the city near the Mori Bastion. Further on, tall chimneys indicate the suburbs of Kishanganj and the Sabzimandi, while the red Mutiny Memorial marks the point of the Ridge.

The other objects noticeable on the Ridge are, in order—a stone pillar of Asoka, the house of Hindu Rāo, the "Observatory," and the Chauburji Mosque (only one of the four domes of which remains); then the red Flagstaff Tower, and, a good distance away, an old ruined artillery hospital. Just below the Ridge, and on the river bank, is a magazine; a white dome indicates the village of Chandrāwal; and lastly appears the waterworks chimney, completing the circuit to Metcalfe House.

From the mound it is possible to realize the peculiar situation of the Ridge with regard to the city. The north face of the walls lies practically at right angles to the river's general course; the Mutiny Memorial is a little over a thousand yards from the corner of the city; but the mound is nearly twice as distant, and yet lies only halfway to the line of the Ridge. It was on account of this obliqueness of the Ridge to the walls that the advanced piquets on this mound, and around

Metcalfe House, had to be thrown forward, in order to command some ravines in front. The Farm piquet was directly in front, and the Cow-house piquet rather to the left—both on the far side of a ravine; while the Stable piquet was half-left, and some six hundred yards further forward, close to a modern house. Across the river, near some trees, the enemy established a battery to fire on the piquets on this side.

Old Cantonments.—The Alipur Road skirts the Metcalfe Park, which lies to the right—old gateways showing where houses used to stand—and crosses the Ridge in a slight cutting, called the "Khyber Pass." On the left was the Sadr Bāzār, or principal bāzār of the cantonments. Across the plain, over which the road runs, there still extends a long line of "bells-of-arms," in which the arms and accoutrements of the sepoys used to be locked up; the officers' houses stood on the near side, the "lines" of sepoys' huts were beyond, and further on still were the parade grounds, abutting on a deep drain, which draws off the water from a swamp at Najafgarh, some miles away. This cut was a great protection to the camp during the siege, running, as it did in that year, nearly full.

About three miles beyond the cantonments

the Alipur Road effects a junction with the old Grand Trunk Road, which, leaving the city by the Lahore Gate, runs under the Ridge, near the Mutiny Memorial, and through the Sabzimandi. The two roads meet near a village, Azādpur; a mile further on is a fortified enclosure, the Badli-ki-Sarāi, at which the rebels first opposed the avenging force in its advance on June 8, 1857. Having fought a successful action, the force was divided into its two brigades at Azādpur, and advanced to the capture of the Ridge by the two roads.

To the right of the Alipur Road, a short distance after it crosses the drain, was a practice-ground of the Sappers and Miners when they were quartered in Dariāganj, some sixty years ago; to the left was a Government Garden (or "Company Bāgh"), and also ice-pits, in which the ice, made during the winter, was stored for summer consumption. On this side also lay the racecourse, and a garden beyond enclosed the house of Sir David Ochterlony, who was Resident in Delhi early in the nineteenth century. The amphitheatre, where the Coronation Durbar was held in 1903, lies, some distance away, to the right of the Alipur Road.

Military Cemetery.—It is but a short

distance, along the bank of the drain, to the old Military Cemetery, in which lies many a victim to shot and shell and disease; among the latter Sir Henry Barnard, who was, for about a month, in command of the besieging force. His first gravestone is built into the wall near the entrance-gate, but his grave is opposite that of Colonel Chester, who was killed by the first discharge of the enemy's guns at Badli-ki-Sarāi.

Flagstaff Tower.—A road to the Flagstaff Tower leads past the modern Viceroy's Circuit-house; on the plain to the right is a mound, called the "General's Mound," which defended the right of the camp. Close to the Flagstaff Tower our troops found more of the enemy posted, and had to fight a second, though short, engagement to dislodge them. This place was also the scene, on the 11th of May, of the concentration of an agitated crowd of women, children, ayahs and other servants, all vainly looking towards the bridge for signs of relief from Meerut; there were no British troops at Delhi. At évening, the few remaining sepoys becoming restless, they fled to Karnāl and Meerut. But the country was up, bands of marauding Gujars (a wild tribe constantly under police surveillance) searched them out, and stripped them even of their clothes;

they staggered along by day in the burning sun, and crouched at night in thickets, trembling at every sound, suffering agonies which can be but faintly imagined. Many were murdered.

About a hundred and fifty yards to the north of the tower is an enclosure, in which rest the remains of four officers of the 54th Bengal Native Infantry. This regiment was ordered down from the Cantonments by the brigadier to quell any riot which might arise from the arrival of the rebels from Meerut. As the regiment debouched from the main-guard enclosure at the Cashmere Gate, a few rebel cavalrymen attacked the officers, and the sepoys did not raise a weapon to interfere, but broke off into the city. The colonel was wounded in seventeen places—some say bayoneted by his own men—but survived until evening, and was carried off in the retreat, never to be heard of again. The bodies of these four officers were recovered and sent up here on a cart, on which they were still lying when our troops regained the Ridge a month later.

Hindu Rāo's House (p. 170).—The position taken up on the afternoon of the 8th of June, after a march of over ten miles in the blazing sun, and after fighting two actions, extended along the Ridge from the Flagstaff Tower to Hindu Rāo's house.

Between these two points are two buildings, the first being the Chauburji Mosque, the other a very old structure, built by Firoze Shāh in the fourteenth century. This, though now named the "Observatory," may have been a hunting-tower, past which the game would be driven to be shot at from the top. To the left of this building may still be traced the remains of a battery; at the further corner of a modern reservoir, and in front of Hindu Rāo's house, was another; while others again were thrown up in the much-quarried ground beyond.

The history of Hindu Rāo's house will be found elsewhere, for it would be a pity to insert here details which might lessen the deep interest in the house, on account of the part it played in the siege. The Mr. Fraser, elsewhere mentioned, was shot at the turn of a road, which ascends the Ridge from the civil lines.

This famous house was held against many a fierce attack by Major Reid, with his Sirmur Gurkhas, some of the 60th Rifles, and the infantry of the Guide Corps, assisted by the 1st Punjab Infantry. In remembrance of their comradeship here, the two first-named regiments wear the same uniform to this day. From this house, riddled through and through with shot and shell, until the verandah columns were knocked to pieces, the Gurkhas never budged, except to pursue the baffled enemy; the wounded, even, refused to be taken to the hospital in the sheltered camp below, for Gurkhas dislike being parted from their wounded. The brunt of most of the attacks fell on the garrison here, and the three first corps had 1011 casualties.

Mutiny Memorial.—Between this house and the Mutiny Memorial there stands, close to the road, a pillar. This was erected at Meerut, in the third century B.C., by King Asoka, to record the result of a great Buddhist conference, and was removed here, sixteen hundred years later, by Firoze Shāh, to grace his hunting-park. This pillar was much injured by a gunpowder explosion, broken into five pieces, and rather roughly put together again; the inscription has become deleted. Another of these pillars stands in the Kotila of Firoze Shāh, a third at Allāhābād, and a fourth is said to have been used as a road-roller at Benāres!

From the Mutiny Memorial, at the end of the Ridge, a most interesting panorama is unrolled. The yellow dome of the church, and the square tank on the mills, near the Mori Bastion, indicate the line of the walls. The Mori Bastion itself, from which such a harassing fire was poured on our batteries, is almost in a line with the minarets of a mosque, far away in Dariāganj. The trees have now grown up, although not sufficiently to hide the bastion, but in 1857 there were very few trees to hide the walls from view, and very few houses in the civil lines, where now there are many.

The nearest of some tall chimneys to the right marks a sarāi, constantly occupied by the enemy, in the suburb of Kishanganj; the Sabzimandi suburb extends from some malt-houses, with queer tops, to some high mill buildings behind the Ridge. Between the two suburbs run the railways, and the canal of Ali Mardān Khān, made in the reign of Shāh Jahān, and called the "Canal of Paradise;" it was cleared and straightened and reopened in 1820. Beyond Kishanganj is the now populous suburb of the Sadr Bāzār, in 1857 a collection of mean hovels, and called Pahāripur; behind this suburb an old Idgāh, a place of worship on Mahomedan festivals, crowns a hill which is the continuation of the Ridge. Beyond a bridge over the canal, and to the right of the road leading down off the Ridge, is a monument to those of the 1st European Bengal Fusiliers, who fell in attacks made on Kishanganj.

Particular notice should be taken of a mass of gardens in the Sabzimandi, among which are the trees of the Roshanāra Bāgh, made by the lady of that name, favourite sister and staunch adherent of Aurangzeb. In these gardens the rebels found fine cover, from which to harass the defences on this part of the Ridge, and also the camp; the operation of driving them out was always costly in lives to both sides, although our men rather enjoyed the "rat-hunting." The drainage-cut is marked by a line of trees, and the General's Mound just shows above the trees on the slope of the Ridge at the back.

It will now be possible, bearing in mind the places already pointed out, to trace the position attained by our force in the first week of September, after nearly three months of struggle. Near the river were the Metcalfe piquets, and the Mound, with a piquet in support at the Flag-staff Tower. At the Mosque was another piquet, and at the "Observatory" the Left Battery with heavy guns. In front of Hindu Rāo's house, and along the Ridge, up to the extreme point where the memorial now stands, were several more heavy gun batteries, not to mention breast-works to guard the intervals. Down the hill, the enclosure of a white-pinnacled temple, called the "Sammy-house," had been occupied, and about three hundred yards to the left of this a battery for light guns had been constructed, in readiness to be armed on the arrival of the siege-train; it was meant to cover the construction of the siege-batteries. A miniature embrasure of red sandstone, marking the site of this light battery, is nearly in line with the church. The defences had also been carried down the reverse slope of the Ridge to a sarāi, marked by an iron chimney, in the Sabzimandi; the Sarāi piquet was posted there. The "Crow's Nest" battery was in this line of works, at the bottom of the slope; it was armed with light mortars, in order to play on the masses of the enemy as they advanced to the attack. Then came a battery on the General's Mound, with light field-guns below in a breast-work; cavalry piquets patrolled beyond, up to the drain, which was usually full of water. On the racecourse in rear, among the bodies of camels, horses, and cattle, was another piquet, and two heavy guns were in battery there. Lastly, the river flank of the camp was watched by cavalry patrols, supported by two light guns.

And now let us pause for a moment at this point, the promontory against which the sea of the enemy's attacks first broke, and consider what our troops had to endure. In June, when they first arrived, the rocks of the Ridge are burning hot, there is a terrific glare, hot winds blow constantly, so that the men could hardly fight, and many dropped with sunstroke. On the 27th of June the tropical rains started, affording some relief from heat, but drenching the men to the bone, and bringing cholera and fever to thin the ranks. All the while they were fighting against numbers at least four times as great, and losing heavily; the memorial records that 2163 officers and men were returned as killed, wounded, and missing between the 8th of June and the 7th of September. The mutineers were frequently reinforced by large numbers; they had at their disposal the largest arsenal in India. "We were the besieged, not the besiegers." But not an inch of ground was ceded, the enemy was never allowed to retain the smallest advantage, cost what it might to drive him back. All honour to those brave men, who by their courage and endurance upheld the prestige of the British arms against a by no means despicable foe, and under climatic conditions which it had always been supposed would make it impossible for British troops to take the field.

Police Lines.—The next objects of interest are the siege-batteries, the first of which was placed where now are the police lines. On the way there the road, as it descends from the Ridge, passes the "Crow's Nest," overhanging a deep pond, opposite the Sarāi piquet. The Mori Bastion also, shattered by constant fire, appears at closer range, as the road passes the "Sammy-house." Bastions, it may be explained, are four-sided works, built out in advance of the main walls, and designed both to fire to the front and to sweep the faces of the "curtains," the technical word for the connecting walls. Where the distance between two bastions was too great for grape-shot to be effective, Martello towers, mounting a single gun, and loopholed at the ground level for musketry, were introduced. These towers were entered by draw-bridges, so that, in the event of a riot in the city, they might be utilized as forts. The bastions and towers were constructed by British engineers, in order to improve the defensible condition of Shāh Jahān's walls, and it was the irony of fate that they were first used against ourselves.

A small red sandstone embrasure in the police lines marks the site of the right half of No. I. Battery, designed to fire on the Mori Bastion. The left half was near a well, visible from the road, in the garden of the house, which is next to the Court of the Sessions Judge. This battery, for a time, fired on the Cashmere Gate, now hidden by trees, but the guns were afterwards removed to the great breaching battery. A ravine runs close by, which afforded shelter to working parties and reliefs passing to and from the camp.

Cemetery.—From a point, where six roads meet, a road leads between a garden, in which is the statue put up in honour of John Nicholson, and a cemetery, where he lies buried; his grave is but a few paces distant from the gate. The joy of those who heard of the fall of Delhi was gone, when they received the news of his death, almost in the moment of victory.

Ludlow Castle.—From the cemetery the Alipur Road runs to the gate of the grounds of Ludlow Castle, now the Delhi Club; near the gate are three more batteries. One is in the garden of a house adjoining the cemetery, close to the wall of the latter; this was the right half of No. II., the great breaching battery. In those days the present dense grove of trees within the cemetery walls did not exist. The left half of this battery was in the grounds of Ludlow Castle, at a somewhat greater range; the miniature embrasure is visible from the road. In the corner of the Kudsia Gardens was No. IV. Battery, armed with heavy mortars, which harassed the enemy, while the breaching batteries battered the walls.

Kudsia Gardens.—A road runs towards the river from opposite the gate of the Ludlow Castle grounds, and this leads to the most interesting battery of all. On the way there it runs through the old Kudsia Bāgh, a name now given to all the grounds here, but up to 1857 confined to a walled garden, of which only the gateway, a corner-tower, and a portion of the walls remain. In front of the gate was a court, with surrounding houses, under the shelter of which No. IV. Battery was constructed. At the south-east corner of the walled garden is an old mosque. From the top of this the rebels kept up an annoying fire one night, while the orange and lime trees were being cleared away, to make room for a battery which Captain Taylor, of the Bengal Engineers, proposed to make behind the garden walls, through which embrasures were to be opened. But, when morning dawned, it was found that a swell in the ground, not noticeable from the top of the wall, would mask the Water Bastion, so a new site had to be sought. Boldly advancing to reconnoitre, Captain Taylor found himself in the "Custom-house," which was the court of the principal Salt-line officer. In those days a thick hedge was maintained for hundreds of miles south of Delhi, to prevent the smuggling of salt (which is taxable) from the Rājputāna States into British India. This building, with its outhouses, seemed just the place, and the general sanctioned the construction of a battery there.

Custom-house Battery.—All traces of the "Custom-house" have disappeared; it was a large and long building, with a verandah on the city side. Between the verandah pillars a sand-bag parapet was made during the first night, so as to hide what was going on, and inside the main room a parapet of earth was thrown up. When all was ready, holes were knocked in the wall, so that the guns might open fire, and the sand-bags in front were removed. But the difficulty of constructing the battery under a heavy fire, and in a position such that a sight could not be taken to the point of attack, had caused an error to be made in the embrasures. It was suggested to the artillery officer that the guns might open fire and put things to rights, but he demurred, so the sappers and miners, with admirable coolness, mounted on the parapet and rearranged the sand-bags in the face of a tremendous fire at short range, and in broad daylight. The whole of the circumstances connected with this battery, from the adventurous reconnaissance, throughout the construction, to this last gallant action, were very remarkable. All was done literally in the face of an undaunted enemy, whose round shot came with such force as to pierce both walls of a room, which it had not been possible to protect, and to kill an artilleryman in the back verandah. And many of the men who worked at this battery were unarmed coolies!

A miniature embrasure on the floor of an outhouse is supposed to mark the site where the left-hand gun was placed, but most of the guns were in the house itself, even further forward, and within a hundred and eighty yards of the walls.

Cashmere Bastion.—An examination of the breaches shows that they were not so very practicable for an assault, and the ruined condition of the Cashmere Bastion makes it possible to imagine the scene during the bombardment and subsequent assault. When all the batteries were at work, on the afternoon of the 12th of September, a tremendous storm of shot and shell fell on the "curtain" between the Water and Cashmere bastions, directed especially to the junctions with the bastions. At the same time the parapets were knocked away as much as possible, so as to deprive the enemy of shelter. The old walls were tough, and it was not until the evening of the 13th that the fire of twenty-four guns and mortars was considered to have had sufficient effect to make it worth while to examine the breaches. At ten o'clock that night firing was suspended, the engineers crept down to reconnoitre, and returned to report practicable breaches.

So, in the dark before the dawn, three columns came down, one behind the "Custom-house," another, under Nicholson, to some thickets in front of the Cashmere Bastion, the third on the road leading to the Cashmere Gate. At the last moment it was discovered that the enemy had been at work, and had partially repaired the breaches, so fire was reopened, and the assault took place in daylight. The 60th Rifles advanced with a cheer, as a signal to the gunners to cease their fire, the ladder-parties and explosion-party ran forward in the face of a rain of bullets, which laid many low, a twenty-foot drop into the ditch was made light of, and the breaches were mounted, while the enemy, having discharged their muskets, hurled bricks and stones, and fought doggedly on. At this moment Home and Salkeld blew in the Cashmere Gate, and the enemy fled. The walls of Delhi had been gained, but the enemy would not leave the city, and night fell, after a long day of fighting, while only the fringe of the city was in our possession.

NOTE.—An account of the siege will be found in Chapter XI.

CHAPTER II

THE PLAINS TO THE SOUTH OF DELHI

Mahomedan kings—Cābul Gate—Lahore Gate—Ajmere Gate—Kutb Road—Jantar Mantar—Tombs of Lodi kings—Safdar Jang's tomb—Panoramas—Kutb Minār—Adjacent buildings—Iron pillar—Shrine of Nizām-ud-din—Humāyun's tomb—Purāna Kila—Kotila of Firoze Shāh—Asoka Pillar.

Map of the Seven Cities, *p.* 132.

THE ancient cities of Delhi (except a portion of one) lay to the south of the modern city, and the monuments which indicate their sites (for the old walls have practically disappeared) are scattered over an area of ground, which measures roughly eleven miles long by five miles wide. These monuments have been erected during a period of time which extends over certainly nine centuries, and some of them have a still greater antiquity, but one difficult to estimate. It is most interesting to trace the evolution of the different architectural styles, which, with the aid of inscriptions, make it possible to judge the period to which a building belongs. Many of these buildings are connected with men whose histories we know, and it will be necessary to mention the kings, whose tombs abound, but not always desirable to fill the description with their dates. It is probably best to insert here a table, showing the kings whose names are closely connected with Delhi, so that the reader may know where to find it. It commences with the Mahomedan conquest, because we are not exactly acquainted with the dates of the Hindu rājas who reigned before that time. The names of contemporary English monarchs have been added, to enable a better realization of the times at which the various kings and emperors ruled India, or at least Delhi.

First Dynasty. The Turks, or "Slaves."

1.	1206.	Kutb-ud-din, slave of Mahomed of Ghor.	John.	1199.
3.	1210.	Altamsh, slave of 1.	Henry III.	1216.
4.	1236.	Firoze Shāh, son of 3.		
5.	1237.	Riziyat, daughter of 3.		
6.	1240.	Bahrām Shāh, son of 3.		
8.	1246.	Māhmud Ghori, son of 3.		
9.	1266.	Balban, slave of 3.	Edward I.	1272.
10.	1287.	Kāi Kubād, son of 9.		

Second Dynasty. Khilji.

1.	1290.	Jalāl-ud-din.		
2.	1296.	Alā-ud-din, son of 1.	Edward II.	1307
4.	1316.	Mubārik, son of 2.		
5.	1320.	Khusru Khān.		

The Plains to the South of Delhi

Third Dynasty. Tughlak Shāhıs.

1.	1320.	Tughlak Shāh.		
2.	1324.	Mahomed Ibn Tughlak, son of 1.	Edward III.	1327.
3.	1351.	Fıroze Shāh, nephew of 1.	Richard II.	1377.
8.	1393.	Māhmud, grandson of 3.	Henry IV.	1399.

Fourth Dynasty. Sāyyads.

1.	1414.	Khizr Khān.	Henry V.	1413.
2.	1421.	Mubārık Shāh, son of 1.	Henry VI.	1422.
3.	1434.	Mahomed Shāh, grandson of 1.		

Fıfth Dynasty. Lodis (Afghāns).

1.	1450.	Bahlol Lodı.	Edward IV.	1461.
			Rıchard III.	1483.
2.	1488.	Sıkandar Lodı, son of 1.	Henry VII.	1485.
3.	1518.	Ibrāhim Lodı, son of 2.	Henry VIII.	1509.

Sixth Dynasty. Moghals.

1.	1526.	Bābar.		
2.	1530.	Humāyun, son of 1.		

Interregnum. Afghāns.

1.	1540.	Sher Shāh drıves out Humāyun.		
2.	1545.	Islām Shāh, son of 1.	Edward VI.	1547.
			Mary.	1553.

Moghal Dynasty resumed.

	1555.	Humāyun returns.		
3.	1556.	Akbar, son of Humāyun.	Elizabeth.	1558.
4.	1605.	Jahāngır, son of 3.	James I.	1603.
5.	1627.	Shāh Jahān, son of 4.	Charles I.	1625.

6.	1658.	Aurungzeb, son of 5, whom he deposed.	Cromwell, Protector.	1653.
			Charles II.	1660
			James II	1685.
			William and Mary	1689.
7.	1707.	Shāh Ālam Bahādur Shāh, son of 6	Anne.	1702.
8.	1712.	Jahāndār Shāh, son of 7		
9.	1713.	Farukhsiyar, nephew of 8.	George I	1714
12.	1719	Mahomed Shāh, cousin of 9	George II.	1727
13.	1748	Ahmad Shāh, son of 12.		
14	1754	Alamgir II, son of 13.		
15.	1759.	Shāh Ālam, son of 14.	George III	1760.
16	1806	Akbar Shāh II, son of 15	George IV.	1820.
			William IV.	1830.
17	1837	Bahādur Shāh, son of 16, and last of the Moghals.	Victoria	1837.

It will be observed that the numbers of the kings of Delhi in their respective dynasties are not consecutive, but all have not been included, for some reigned a very short time, and have little to do with the monuments at Delhi. The comparative table is distinctly interesting, for it shows that in our own history kings have succeeded each other as quickly as those of Delhi.

Domes are a very prominent feature in both Hindu and Mahomedan architecture; it is at times doubtful whether they surmount a mosque, or a tomb, or even a Hindu temple. The two latter have each one dome, a pyramidal one in the case of the temple, but a mosque has (with very rare exceptions) three or more domes. A Hindu temple is also distinguishable by the fact that a small flag on a bamboo pole flies over it.

There are several routes to the plains, south of Delhi, from the civil lines; but the best is that which avoids the crowded bāzārs, and follows the Circular Road *viâ* the Cābul Gate.

Cābul Gate.—This gate, close to which John Nicholson was mortally wounded, is now filled by an earthen ramp, which takes the Queen's Road over the railway. Turning to the left at the top of the ramp the road passes the Teliwāra Martello Tower, and, shortly afterwards, the Burn Bastion. From a gap in the wall, caused by the removal of the Lahore Gate, a road over the railway leads to the Sadr (or chief) bāzār, which has sprung up since 1857, and has developed into an enormous suburb. Beyond the railway is a branch of the Western Jumna Canal, which connects with another canal, flowing down to and beyond Agra, from a weir at Okhla. This branch was, until recently, used for navigation; this use of canals is now discountenanced in India, so that its chief purpose is the passing on of surplus water to the Agra Canal. This will give some idea of the way in which water is fully utilized in India.

Lahore Gate.—The Lahore Gate was the limit of the operations during the siege of 1857, and was one of the last points captured—not without difficulty. Inside the gate is the great grain bāzār of Delhi, leading to the Chāndni Chouk.

A mosque which stands outside the gate was built by the Sirhindi Begam, one of the wives whom Shāh Jahān married after the death of his wife, Arjamand Bānu Begam, Mumtāz Mahal.

The walls beyond date back to the days of Shāh Jahān; but they were put in repair, and the defences brought up to date, in the early years of the last century. The Garstin Bastion, then constructed, has been removed to make room for the railway, and gaps have been made in many other places.

Ajmere Gate.—The Ajmere Gate is probably still in much the same condition as when built out of materials borrowed from an older city. Just opposite the gate, and protected by an out-work, built in 1811, is the college of Ghāzi-ud-din, father of the first Nizām of Hyderābād. The school has an endowment, but also receives Government aid. On the west of the college is the founder's tomb and a mosque; outside the ditch are remains of the underground apartments of Safdar Jang, once one of the sights of Delhi.

The Plains to the South of Delhi

Kutb Road.—A road crosses the railway opposite the Ajmere Gate, and joins a road leading to the Kutb Minār; this at first runs through mean streets, and then past some gardens, rather different in their arrangement to those of the West. Then the road passes between some mounds, which are native brick-kilns.

Jantar Mantar (p. 131).—At the third milestone there appears on the left a curious group of buildings, the observatory of Maharāja Jāi Singh, of Jāipur, who constructed them, at the bidding of the Emperor Mahomed Shāh, about the beginning of the eighteenth century. There are here a masonry gnomon, which threw its shadow on a marble dial (long since gone), a small altitude meter, and two round amphitheatres, in which directions and heights of stars could be observed. Some have stigmatized this group as a "folly," and the rustic name of "Jantar Mantar," an alliterative corruption of "Semrāt Yantar," has possibly lent colour to this view; but it is a scientific work which demands respect.

Tombs of Lodi Kings (p. 128).—On the right are low hills, which are the continuation of the Ridge, and run right away through Rājputāna, as far as the Nerbudda River. Further on, a branch juts out to the east, and on part of this is situated Old Delhi, towards which the road is leading. At the fifth milestone four buildings, all domed, come into view on the left. That nearest to modern Delhi is the mausoleum of Sikandar Lodi, the next that of Ibrāhim Lodi, while a fine, high dome among trees is above a gateway to a small mosque close by. Last of all, close to a cross-road, is a tomb of an earlier king—Mahomed Shāh, of the Sāyyad dynasty. All are over four hundred years old.

Safdar Jang's Tomb.—There now appears, on the right, a building of considerable size, but comparatively modern, which is the mausoleum of Nawāb Mansur Ali Khān, commonly called Safdar Jang, Prime Minister of Ahmad Shāh and nephew of the man who founded the House of Oudh. The title of "Safdar Jang" means "Disperser of the battle ranks," but on more than one occasion it was his own that he dispersed, by ignominious flight.

The building follows rather the bad principle of "constructing ornament" than of "ornamenting construction:" there is a too free use of plaster. It is sixty feet square and ninety feet high, surmounted by a marble dome, which is, unfortunately, bulbous and heavy. It stands on a high terrace, in an enclosed garden, and the view of it through the gateway is, like all such views, an effective one. It was the last large mausoleum to be erected near Delhi, and cost thirty thousand pounds sterling. Safdar Jang's successors were independent of Delhi, and preferred to be buried at Lucknow.

Mujāhidpur.—On the left of the road, shortly after it leaves this tomb, is the tomb of Najaf Khān, the only brave man and good general that the declining days of the Moghal Empire knew. Then appear various buildings, which are best described in a panoramic view, at the fourth furlong after leaving mile seven, just before the road reaches a small village, Mujāhidpur.

To the right, near a white building among some trees, is a pale dome on the mausoleum of Firoze Shāh; then appears, further away, a dargāh, or shrine, in Mahomedpur. Across the road, at some distance, the marble dome of Humāyun's tomb stands up; another dome, with small pavilions around and on the top, among some trees, marks the tomb of a Sāyyad king, Mubārik Shāh, who died nearly five hundred years ago. Lastly, there is the Moth-ki-Masjid, a mosque with the usual three domes. The other buildings are of little interest.

Mile Nine.—At mile nine from Delhi, and two from the Kutb Minār, the tomb of Firoze

Shāh is still on the left, further round of course; a mile behind, and close to the road, there is a group of nameless tombs, near Mujāhidpur. On the other side of the road is a ruined Idgāh, and also a curious tower with holes, into which were built the heads of captives. Some trees, half hidden by the mounds which encircle them, indicate the ruined city of Siri, founded about the year 1303, by Alā-ud-din, while other still more distant trees, surrounded by walls, mark the enclosure of Roshan Chirāgh Delhi. The circuit is completed by the village of Begampur, with two large, dark, many-domed mosques, and a building close by, raised high on a mound, is called the Bedi Mandal (p. 113); this is said to be of great antiquity. Just one furlong ahead the road has a slight rise, and here were the walls of Jahānpanāh, made to join the city of Siri to Old Delhi; their remains extend towards the Kutb Minār, which has been for some time occasionally discernible between the trees bordering the road.

At mile ten, just where there is a garden, a sharp rise in the road marks the line of the walls of Old Delhi, dating back many centuries, certainly over eight. Some low mounds within the walls are, probably, the remains of houses of mud, built each on the site of former houses, which the tropical rains had dissolved. On the left is a

KUTB MINĀR.

[To face p. 49.

tomb, picturesquely situated on an outcrop of rock, and then, suddenly, above some trees there towers the great Kutb Minār.

Close to the path, which leads to the minār, there stands, on a mound, a red sandstone pavilion, which formerly crowned the tower, but was taken down in 1848, as an eyesore. Near this is a grave—that of a subaltern of H.M. 82nd Regiment, who died of cholera in 1862, while on the march to Gurgāon.

Kutb Minār (p. 88).—The Kutb Minār is over 238 feet in height, but feet and inches convey little impression of height, which can best be gauged by comparison with familiar objects. It is nearly eighty feet higher than the Nelson Column in Trafalgar Square; if erected on the floor of St. Paul's Cathedral, a few feet would project into the lantern of the dome. It was started in A.D. 1200, under the auspices of Kutb-ud-din I-bak, Viceroy of the conqueror of India, some five hundred years before Wren's magnificent work was undertaken.

Other features are bands of writing around, carved flutings, carried in varied design through three stories, and the excellently conceived designs of the carvings on the underside of the balconies. It has more than once been damaged by lightning and earthquake, but sustained no ill effect from the earthquake of 1905, which was felt somewhat severely in Delhi.

The red sandstone, with which it is faced, cannot be obtained nearer than Agra. The marble in the two topmost stories was, probably, a later addition, in the time of Firoze Shāh, and came from Makrānā, hundreds of miles away. These facts may give some idea of the cost of this great monument.

An ascent of 379 steps to the top discloses a great panorama, which, however, is better observed from the first balcony, which affords freer movement. The first glance is naturally directed towards modern Delhi, where the white domes of the Jāma Masjid gleam through the haze, ten miles away, almost in a line with the dome of Safdar Jang's tomb. Then the white marble dome of Humāyun's tomb catches the eye, and, to the right of this, the mosque at Begampur and the Bedi Mandal are prominent. Next, two white domes almost in a line mark, the nearer the shrine of Roshan Chirāgh Delhi, the further a Hindu temple of Kālikā, on a hill. In a grove of trees, towards which an earthen wall extends, is the mosque of Khirki, well worthy of an inspection, but somewhat out of the way. The line of a broad road points almost directly to a marble dome over the tomb of Tughlak Shāh, near his city of Tughlukābād; this city was built, nearly six hundred years ago, of massive stones, some of which weigh several tons. Just to the right of this city is the fort of Adilābād, built on a hill by Tughlak's son, who is buried with him. Close under the minār now, and to the right, is an old tomb, converted into a country residence by Sir Thomas Metcalfe, in 1844, but burnt, like his other house, in 1857. In a line with the ruined house is the Jamāli Masjid, slightly to the left of which is the ruined tomb of Balban. From the other side of the balcony the tomb of Adham Khān is very conspicuous, built on the walls of Old Delhi, while among some trees to the left of this is the shrine of a Mahomedan saint, Kutb-ud-din.

Close under the minār there is the square court, surrounded by cloisters, of the first mosque to be built in Delhi, the Kuwwat-ul-Islām; an iron pillar stands in the court, and a fine row of arches marks the front of the mosque proper, which occupied the western portion. This line of arches was afterwards extended on both sides, and outer colonnades were added, up to a line indicated by a small portion still standing outside the eastern entrance to the court of the mosque. The ruins of a second very large minaret, carried up to the height of eighty feet and then abandoned, show on what scale a further extension of the mosque was planned by Alā-ud-din, who died before he could completely carry out his plans. He was able, however, to add a gateway, which is close to the Kutb Minār, and some colonnades, which extend to the east of it. At one end of the line of arches is the tomb of this king, at the further end that of Altamsh, builder of the first additions to the mosque.

From the balcony can be traced the walls of four cities. First of all, some walls start from the tomb of Adham Khān, and can easily be followed to a commanding bastion, where they stop abruptly, but were once continued to the road, which runs to Tughlukābād : these bounded the citadel of Old Delhi, which was first made about the middle of the eleventh century, by a Hindu rāja, and was restored or improved by the Mahomedans. From the north-west angle of the citadel, the outer wall of the city ran across to the garden, which was passed on the road, a mile away; after that it is only traced with some difficulty, though never more than a mile distant. The Jamāli Mosque, however, stands near the line, which becomes more distinct as it approaches Adham Khān's tomb, and completes the circuit. What look like light sand-hills to the north are the remains of one wall of Jahānpanāh, the "refuge of the world," built to join up the walls of Siri, two miles away, to those of the old city; the wall on the other side of Jahānpanāh runs from a clump of trees which surround the Lado Sarāi, towards the village of Khirki. This wall also served as a dam, to hold up water for the needs of the cities. We have thus traced the walls of Old Delhi, Siri, Jahānpanāh, and Tughlukābād.

Alāi Gateway (p. 92).—Near the foot of the minār is the entrance gateway of Alā-ud-din, built in 1310. This is an example of the beautiful ornamentation, in which the early Mahomedan rulers delighted, but which gave way later to severe designs: the blending of marble and red sandstone in the exterior decoration, the pierced screens to the windows, the diaper pattern inside, all remind one of the decoration of the palace of the Alhambra at Granāda, built over a century later. But, while the Moors had to be content with stucco, the work here is in stone, and very much more effective.

Tomb of Imām Zāmin (p. 93).—Close to the gate is the square tomb of the Imām Zāmin; this dates from the middle of the sixteenth century, and was possibly copied from other tombs of similar design, which may be found on the plains within the limits of Jahānpanāh.

Mosque (p. 94).—The Kuwwat - ul - Islām, or strength of Islam, Mosque is now unused; it is entered from the east by a short flight of steps, the original ones leading to a Hindu temple, which once occupied this site. Those who have seen the beautiful Jain temples of Dilwāra, on Mount Ābu, will perceive the resemblance in the arrangement of the pillars, which divide the roof of the surrounding colonnades into small compartments, each section being differently ornamented. The old Mahomedan kings, while they could not approve of the carving of images, prohibited by their Korān, were quite willing to use the materials of Hindu temples to build their mosques: there are examples of this at Ajmere, in the "Arhāi din ki Jhonpri" Mosque, and at Mahāban, about six miles from Muttra. But the figure carvings were defaced, and covered with plaster, which has now fallen off: fortunately some figures were left intact, especially those in two raised rooms at the corners. It may be mentioned that the prohibition against the making of images is not taken so seriously in these days, for the ivory miniature paintings of Delhi are done by Mahomedan artists. These pillars are

Archæological Photo Works, Delhi.] IRON PILLAR AND GREAT ARCHES.

[*To face p.* 55.

certainly eight hundred years old, but are not in their original positions, having been rearranged by the Mahomedans.

Iron Pillar (p. 96).—In the court of the mosque is that most interesting object, the Iron Pillar, nearly twenty-four feet long, and a marvellous piece of forging, weighing about six tons; such a piece of work would not have been possible in Europe in the days in which it was made, or indeed until many centuries after, for the age of this pillar may be as much as sixteen centuries. It has often been doubted whether the material is really iron, and not a mixture of metals, for one would have thought that it would long ago have rusted away, but analysis has shown it to be composed of pure malleable iron. It is not a natural phenomenon, as the ornamented top will show; a dent made by a cannon-ball, fired at it, so tradition says, by Ghulām Kādir, shows that the workmanship is good, for the blow was only sufficient to crack the pillar.

Great Arches (p. 97).—The central arch, behind the Iron Pillar, was restored by the orders of Lord Mayo, Viceroy of India from 1869 to 1872, in which year he fell by an assassin's hand in the Andaman Islands, the penal settlement of India, to which offenders are transported across the "Black water." Behind the line of arches used to be the covered mosque, but only a few pillars remain, supported by various expedients; the "kiblāh-gāh," or place turned to at prayer, has completely disappeared, and a path runs over the site. Behind this have been excavated some turquoise-coloured tiles, and it is supposed that here stood the "Blue Palace" of an early Mahomedan king.

Tomb of Altamsh (p. 97).—A detour to the right leads to the tomb of Shams-ud-din Altamsh, second Mahomedan king of India, who died in 1236: there is no other tomb anywhere extant of earlier date. The carving of the interior is exquisite, and in very much the same style as that of the work on the great arches; it was probably carried out by the same artisans, or by their pupils. A triple prayer-niche on the west is specially beautiful, but marble cannot have been considered of great account in those days, for traces of painting are still clear on the carving at the top. The tomb is roofless, and it cannot be stated with certainty if it ever possessed one, but it is doubtful if they could have undertaken a dome of twenty-eight feet span in those days. Not the least of the difficulties would have been the centerings: Tavernier states that the centerings of the tomb of Tāj Mahal, at Agra, cost as much as the rest of the building.

Tomb of Adham Khān. — The tomb of Adham Khān stands on the line of the walls of Old Delhi; it is now used as a rest-house for officials. Adham Khān was a foster-brother of the Great Akbar, and the manner of his death is told elsewhere, on p. 220.

The building is octagonal, with an exterior colonnade; sloping minarets buttress the corners, and are continued above. It is not in the least of the type common in the sixteenth century, when it was built, but rather belongs to the style of a hundred years previously: may it have been the grave of one of Adham Khān's ancestors? In the thickness of the walls below the dome is a sort of labyrinth.

Jumping Well.—Not far from this tomb is a stone-lined well, which is adorned with Hindu columns, and into which adventurous divers jump; since the notice, given by these men to visitors, conveys a reproach to writers of books on Delhi, it shall be reprinted here. The language of this notice is decidedly curious—

"One curious seen is in Kutb Minar more, this seen is not written in any guide book, Curious seen Jumping well is too deep from

Fathapur Sakari Agra and Nizam-ud-din Delhi, this well is near the Adam Khan's Tomb Delhi 80 feet deep from ground and 20 feet water 5 minute walk from Kutab Minar and 2 minute drive from Kutub Minar."

Beyond this well, and down the hill, lies the village of Mahrāuli, with the shrine of Kutb-ud-din, which is described elsewhere (p. 99); the shrine of Nizām-ud-din is more important.

Our steps must be retraced to the tomb of Safdar Jang, for the route by Tughlukābād is too long; it will be interesting also to note again the boundaries of the three old cities of Old Delhi, Jahānpanāh, and Siri.

Tomb of Mahomed Shāh (p. 128).—Close to a cross-road, which leads from Safdar Jang's tomb to Humāyun's tomb, lies one of the tombs previously noticed—that of Mahomed Shāh, the Sāyyad king. The style is very much that of Adham Khān's tomb. The tombs of the Lodi kings lie beyond.

Shrine of Nizām-ud-din (p. 114).—The road crosses the Agra-Delhi Railway near a small station, and, shortly afterwards, a road to the right leads to the portal of a dingy-looking group of buildings. Inside is a dark-plastered reservoir of green water, flanked by old tombs, from the top

JAMĀT KHĀNA MOSQUE.

SHRINE OF KHWĀJA NIZĀM-UD-DIN.

TOMBSTONE OF JAHĀNĀRA BEGAM.

TOMB OF TAGA KHĀN.

[*To face p.* 50.

of which boys leap into the water for the ever-solicited "bakshish." But, after passing through tortuous, dusty passages, there breaks on the view a very different picture. In front is the Dargāh, or shrine, of Khwāja Nizām-ud-din Auliā, who lived in the days of Tughlak Shāh, and is reputed to have constantly been on bad terms with that monarch, even to have compassed his death.

On the west of the shrine is a mosque, built by Firoze Shāh six hundred years ago, the principal object of interest in which is a golden bell, hanging from the dome, well out of reach—the Jāts are said to have tried in vain to shoot it down for plunder. The square, domed, marble shrine is beautiful, both outside and in, a special feature being a canopy over the grave, inlaid with mother-of-pearl; this is seen only with difficulty, for the boots must be removed before entering. The grave is, as usual, covered with a pall, there is a prayer-niche, and the pierced marble screens, if not so beautiful as those in the tomb of Salim Chisti, at Fatehpur Sikri, are elegant and costly.

Near by there are three marble enclosures; the first that of Jahānāra Begam, daughter of Shāh Jahān, and sharer of his captivity. The grass on her grave is planted there in compliance with her request, inscribed on the inlaid marble headstone, "Except with grass and green things, let not my grave be covered, for grass is all-sufficient pall for the graves of the poor." The other graves in this enclosure are those of unimportant Moghal princelings.

In the next enclosure lies Mahomed Shāh, in whose reign India was invaded by Nādir Shāh. The victor's son received in marriage one of the king's relatives, but she died in childbirth, and, with her baby, lies here. The marble doors of the enclosure are carved in relief.

In the third enclosure was buried the son of Akbar the Second, Mirzā Jahāngir, who, for firing a pistol at the British Resident, was banished to Allāhābād. There he died, in 1821, of the effects of too much cherry-brandy, to which beverage he was extremely partial, complaining only that it too soon made him intoxicated. The gravestone of the prince is shaped on the top like that of a woman, for that of a man should have a raised pen-box; the explanation of this is, that this stone had already been carved for the grave of some lady, but was thought otherwise very suitable, and a pen-box was fashioned of plaster, which has now disintegrated.

Chausath Khamba.—In another court are

some fine old trees, said to be as old as the shrine itself. Here is the grave of a famous poet, Abul Hassan, or Amir Khusrau, a friend of the saint; the other graves are of little importance, although said to include that of Khondamir, a historian, but this cannot be identified. To the east of the shrine of the saint is the mausoleum of Shams-ud-din Mahomed, Taga Khān, Azam Khān, the foster-father and Prime Minister of Akbar, who conferred on him the titles which make his name so long. The mausoleum was erected by his son, Mirzā *Aziz* Kokaltāsh, governor of several provinces under Akbar; he also built a marble "Chausath Khamba," or Hall of sixty-four pillars, which is close by, and where he himself is buried. His gravestone is near the entrance gate; it is of marble, all in one piece, and valued at Rs.2000. The whole building, pillars, roofs, and screens, is of marble.

Humāyun's Tomb.—From a junction of the road from Safdar Jang's tomb with the Muttra Road, a short road leads to the tomb of Humāyun, passing on the way the mausoleum of Isa Khān; this building is a little more elaborate than that of Adham Khān, and rather similar to the tomb of Mubārik Shāh; it has pavilions on the roof. Isa Khān lived about the middle of the sixteenth century. Then the road skirts a garden, on the walls of which are pavilions, decorated with encaustic tiling, and crosses the old Moghal Road, which ran through the gate of the Arab Sarāi, and may be traced towards the north. The Arab Sarāi was built by Akbar's mother, and is so called because it was the habitation of some three hundred Arabs, whom she may have brought back from Mecca.

The walled enclosure of Humāyun's tomb has two entrances, one to the west, the other on the south; but the former is the principal one. It may be noted that the mosque, usual accompaniment of a tomb, is therefore absent. The mausoleum itself, while it cannot pretend to the delicate, ever-varying beauty of the tomb of Tāj Mahal, at Agra, is yet no mean receptacle for the bones of a king, whose life was rather spent in war than in peace. It must be remembered that the country had hardly been settled, and that the fame of the "Great Mogul" had not then attracted European artists. The ground plan, a square with an irregular octagon at each corner, may have served as a model for the designer of "the Tāj;" the general plan of that building differs only in having regular octagons at the corners. Of course, the material and workmanship there are magnificent, while here both are rough; but then Humāyun's tomb is that of a man. The dome has a constricted neck, foreshadowing the bulbous domes of a later fashion, but it is formed in the old style. The copper pinnacle is 140 feet above the level of the terrace.

On the left of the steps, which lead up to the platform from the western side, is a marble grave, which holds the decapitated body of Dāra Shikoh, eldest son of Shāh Jahān, defeated by Aurangzeb, and murdered not far from here by his orders. Elsewhere on the platform, and in the rooms of a lower story, are the graves of many a scion of the House of Timur. And here was captured the last king, and also his three descendants, who were shot by Hodson.

Across the river a grove of trees marks Patparganj, between which and modern Delhi was fought, in 1803, a decisive battle by Lord Lake against the Mahrattas, then in possession of the imperial city. Their total defeat ended in the first entry of British soldiers into Delhi, on the 14th of September—significant date.

Two small tombs lie towards the south-east; one has a blue-tiled dome, and is said to contain the bones of one Fahim Khān; the other, of red sandstone, is reputed to be the tomb of a favourite barber of Humāyun. A massive tomb, to the south-west, is that of the Khān Khānān, son of Bahrām Khān, Akbar's great general and minister; the marble, which once covered the dome of this tomb, was sold to Asaf-ud-daulah, Nawāb of Oudh, by Shāh Ālam, for the sum of Rs.25,000.

The upper floor of Humāyun's tomb is practically level with the terrace; the real grave, as usual, is below, a cenotaph being placed on the floor above to indicate the site. In 1611, the floor was covered with rich carpets, and a magnificent ceiling-cloth was suspended over the cenotaph; beside copies of the Korān on reading-stands, were still kept the sword, dagger, and shoes of the monarch, who had died in 1556. All these relics have disappeared, and unsightly whitewash has disfigured the interior.

Purāna Kila (p. 127).—Between Humāyun's tomb and Shāhjahānābād lie monuments which indicate the site of two more ancient cities, covering to some extent the same ground. Here also is the "Purāna Kila," or old fort of Humāyun, persistently alleged by the Hindus to be on the site of Indraprastha, and therefore called "Indarpat." The modern road, which leads to the gate, passes, at some distance on the right, a fortified enclosure, said to have been the residence of Humāyun's barber, but possibly a palace of that monarch himself. Between this enclosure and the old fort there stands a pillar, one of the "Kos minārs" or two-mile stones, on the old imperial Delhi-Agra road.

Opposite a turning, which leads to the fort, is a mosque in a cloistered enclosure, attributed to Māham Anāgāh, one of the foster-mothers of Akbar; she founded a college here. A red gate and battlements near by indicate the southern limits of the city of Sher Shāh, built about 1541.

Kila Kona Mosque (p. 127).—The entrance gate of the "Purāna Kila" is a very fine one, with varied decoration of black and yellow stone among the red. There is a slit over the gate, suggestive of boiling oil or molten lead, and tiles adorn the balconies above. The interior of the walls is filled with squalid houses, but contains a very fine mosque, called "Kila Kona" (at the corner of the fort), with very effective, many-coloured decoration on the front, and an interior which reminds one of the fine mosque at Fatehpur Sikri. There is only one dome left out of three; the other two had to be removed; years ago. The earthquake of 1905 cracked the southern wall badly.

Not far from here is an octagonal, three-storied, red sandstone building called the "Sher

Mandal," built by Sher Shāh, for an unknown purpose, but used by Humāyun as a library; here the latter met his death, by accidentally falling down the inconveniently steep stairs.

Outside the gate of the fort, near a large tree, is a platform, close to the old road, and on this Hodson is said—probably quite erroneously—to have made the three princes stand when he shot them; it is said that a number of armed men emerged from the fort, and that their threatening attitude caused him to take the decision to do so.

Kotila of Firoze Shāh (p. 123).—To the left of the road, after it leaves the "Purāna Kila," lie the ruins of the city of Firozābād, built by Firoze Shāh. The Kotila, or citadel, of that monarch is opposite the modern jail, near which is the Cābul Gate of Sher Shāh's city. On the top of a much-ruined three-storied building, now stripped of its facing walls, stands a most interesting object: one of the Pillars of Asoka, nearly twenty-two centuries old. This was brought here by Firoze Shāh, in 1357, from its first site, near the Sewālik Hills, and was set up on this specially erected building; a ball and crescent of gold were fitted to the top of the pillar, the inscriptions on which are still quite plain.

ASOKA PILLAR.

To face p. 67.

Close to the pillar is the Jāma Masjid of Firoze Shāh, now in ruins, and despoiled of the massive monolithic pillars which supported the vaulted roofs of colonnades around the central court. A very good idea of what the mosque looked like in former days can be obtained from the Kalān, or Great, Mosque (p. 122), within the Turkmān Gate of the city. To the south of this Jāma Masjid was the palace of Firoze Shāh, now an utter ruin.

And now the road leads to the Delhi Gate of Shāhjahānābād. It is called by that name because it opens towards the old cities of Delhi, the positions of which have been clearly indicated in this chapter. In the next we shall endeavour to trace the reasons for the frequent changes of site.

CHAPTER III

THE SEVEN CITIES OF DELHI

The traditional Indraprastha—Hindu history—Hindu rājas—Mahomedan conquest—The seven cities—Dates and circumstances of their foundation—Reasons for successive abandonment—Vagaries of the river—Climatic conditions altered.

Map of the Seven Cities of Delhi, p. 132.

THE plains to the south of the modern city of Delhi certainly present an extraordinary aspect. In fact, we have only to imagine London deserted, the houses pulled down, and the materials removed; St. Paul's Cathedral, the Nelson Column in Trafalgar Square, and a few other buildings standing in solitary grandeur; hamlets scattered about here and there; and we have some idea of the havoc which has been wrought. The walls of Old Delhi and of Tughlukābād, it is true, have not been entirely removed; but of the other four cities next to nothing remains to show their limits. Much the same thing may be seen at Old Goa, where churches stand scattered about on a plain, without a house at hand to shelter a worshipper.

It may well be asked, "Why did they abandon a city which had been surrounded by walls, and was therefore secure; why pull down those walls to build others not so very far off?" Many a city in India still occupies the same site which it has occupied for many a century; at least, the inhabitants have but very slightly shifted their houses. The explanation of this will be attempted later; but first let us consider the seven cities of Delhi in the order in which they were built.

If Hindu tradition is to be believed, the city of Indraprastha, sung of in the great Indian epic, the "Mahābharata," was situated on these plains; over the possession of this city were waged the wars, described in such detail in that tremendous poem, in comparison with which the "Iliad" of Homer and the "Æneid" of Virgil shrink to small dimensions. Strange to say, this earliest city also is said to have been abandoned by the Pandus, headed by King Yudisthira; and their reason for doing so was that, one day, when the cover of a dish was removed, the king found on the food a fly. Dwellers in modern Delhi would not consider this a matter of importance—indeed, find it an everyday occurrence; but the king saw in this impertinence of a small insect a hint that the glory had departed, and at once abandoned the city, to perish in the Himālayas. The natives of Delhi have for years believed, and still believe, that the "Purāna Kila" occupies the site of Indraprastha; but on what facts this tradition may be founded cannot be stated. Most writers on the subject of Delhi appear, if somewhat doubtfully, to have accepted this tradition, although rejecting the idea that the walls of "Purāna Kila" belong to Hindu times, which they certainly do not. At least one writer goes further, and accepts the modern tradition that the Nigambodh Ghāt of the "Mahābharata" was situated outside the Nigambodh Gate of Shāhjahānābād. But there is every reason to believe that this site, not so many centuries ago, was covered by the waters of the Jumna. That the city of Indraprastha stood on the traditional site is not altogether impossible, as will be seen; but there is no sign to-day of such a city. The probable date of its foundation, wherever it may have stood, was 1450 B.C.

Hindu history is practically non-existent, for we are now in the epoch known as the Iron Age, the deeds performed in which are not considered worthy of record; all we have are certain inscriptions on pillars or copper-plates, and these usually concern themselves only with religious matters, such as the resolutions of Buddhist councils, or grants of land to temples. The earliest mention of Delhi, as a city of that name, occurs in the songs of Hindu bards; there is a story, in one of these lays, of the site having been abandoned for 792 years before it was repeopled. We know, from an inscription on the Iron Pillar, that "Ang Pāl built Delhi in A.D. 1052," but the best authorities give to the pillar itself an antiquity which extends to the third or fourth century of the Christian era: this conclusion is obtained by the form of the writing of the earliest inscription on the pillar. A century, more or less, does not matter much, and the difference of these two figures, 1052 and (say) 300, is not so very far out from 792, all things considered, so the Hindu bard may have sung correctly. The presence of the Iron Pillar argues that the city really had been previously occupied, for the pillar is so heavy that it cannot be far from the place where it was first set up. It is possible, therefore, that the word translated as "built" should be rendered "rebuilt." But when we turn to ancient historians for light on this point, we find them silent.

The Greek historians, who took their accounts from those who accompanied Alexander the

Great in 327 B.C., mention Muttra, but not Delhi, or any name like it: the historians were, it is true, only able to obtain hearsay evidence, for Alexander was not able to march further than the Hyphasis (the modern Beās); but this goes to show the unimportance of Delhi at that time. One suggestive remark by Arrian, who got his information from Megasthenes, an ambassador of Seleucus (the successor of Alexander), to Chandra Gupta, King of Magadha or Behār, must be quoted; this has to do with the question of the abandonment of traditional Indraprastha. He says, "Such cities as are situated on the banks of rivers . . . are built of wood, instead of stone, so destructive are the heavy rains, which pour down, and the rivers also, when they overflow their banks and inundate the plains."

Between 181 and 161 B.C., India was invaded by Græco-Bactrian armies, and mention is made of Muttra as one of the places taken; but there is not a word of Delhi, although it must have lain in the route to the former place. Three Chinese pilgrims visited India, between A.D. 390 and 645, to visit the Buddhist shrines, among which those at Muttra were prominent; but there is not a single mention in their writings of Delhi. This, however, may only prove that Delhi was not a stronghold of Buddhism, for only those places find record. Nevertheless, the last pilgrim, Hwen Thsang, must have passed close to the site of Delhi, for he retraced his steps from Muttra to Thanesar, and, had Delhi been a very large or important city, he would surely have taken some notice of it. Again, we have accounts of India dating from about A.D. 1000, when Māhmud of Ghazni invaded the country, sacked Kanāuj and Muttra, and other places of importance; but there is no mention of Delhi, which cannot have been a tempting prey for the rapacious invader.

We may, therefore, with some confidence suppose (and it is generally agreed) that Delhi was first occupied somewhere about the year A.D. 300, that the city was afterwards abandoned, for some cause which we do not know, and that it was not repeopled until A.D. 1052, after the final retirement of Māhmud of Ghazni. Anang Pāl was a Tuār, which tribe had been forced to leave Kanāuj, which was sacked by Māhmud; possibly it was this forced migration which led him to think of Delhi as his new capital. He must, however, have had a considerable force at his disposal, for Delhi lay direct in the route of foreign invaders, the incursions of whom were still fresh in men's minds, although they had for the time being ceased.

In Old Delhi the Tuār kings, Anang Pāl and his successors, reigned undisturbed, as we may suppose, for a century, during which time they were able to build the city walls, and construct certain masonry dams and tanks, about eight miles to the south-east: it is true that the reputed dates of these works would make their construction date from about the middle of the eighth century, but this can be explained by a mistake in the era from which the dates are counted. In A.D. 1151 there was an irruption of Chohān Rājputs, who conquered Delhi, but an arrangement was come to, by which the Tuār should marry a Chohān princess, and their offspring be King of Delhi. We have evidence of this Chohān conqueror in an inscription on the pillar of Asoka, which stands in the Kotila of Firoze Shāh: this inscription is dated A.D. 1164, and records the power of Visala Deva, whose kingdom extended from the Himalaya mountains to the Vindhya Range, bordering the Nerbudda River. This king probably was the grandfather of Prithwi Rāja, who built the citadel of Lālkot, in Old Delhi, and who, after once defeating the Mahomedan invaders, in his turn met with adverse fortune, being killed by them in 1193 on the battlefield of Tilauri. And so Old Delhi passed into Mahomedan hands, and became the capital of the invaders; here the first Mahomedan kings of India ascended the throne, and erected those monuments, prominent among which is the wonderful Kutb Minār. We must presume that Delhi was then the most important Hindu city, at all events in this part of India, for twenty-seven temples had been built within its limits; it was retained as their principal city by the victorious Mahomedans.

A century later, the confined area of Old Delhi was not able to accommodate the growing population, and suburbs stretched out into the plains to the north-east. A great horde of Moghals now invaded India, penetrated as far as Delhi, and plundered the defenceless suburbs. Alā-ud-din, therefore, in 1303, had to entrench his army at Siri to cover them, and, when the Moghals retired, he there constructed the second city.

In A.D. 1320, Tughlak Shāh came to the throne, the whole of the princes of the previous dynasty having disappeared. He was a stern old warrior, accustomed to the constant attacks of enemies whom he had met in the frontier province, where he had been "Warden of the Marches," and he was not content with the comparatively low walls of Old Delhi, which gave less security than he considered desirable. So he built a city, five miles to the eastward, round a rocky hill, which gave the isolation which he required. Rocky hills, however, do not give facilities for obtaining water, and, although reservoirs might store a certain amount for emergencies, nevertheless the inhabitants would prefer to remain in the plains, where wells or tanks could easier supply their wants. The traditional cause for the desertion of Tughlukābād is a curse uttered against the place by the saint Nizām-ud-din. He was engaged, at the time of the building of the city, in building his own dwelling, and we may suppose that the king wanted every mason available, at all events he forbade them to work for the saint. The latter had to get them to work for him at night; but the king heard of it, and ordered that no oil should be supplied to him. This difficulty was got over by the use of his miraculous powers, but the saint was very much annoyed, and cursed the new city. "May it remain deserted, or may it be a habitation for Gujars," said he; and in that state is Tughlukābād to this day.

The large population, which resided on the open plain between Old Delhi and Siri, was naturally in a very insecure position, and so Mahomed Tughlak, second of the dynasty, found it necessary to construct walls to join up the two

WALLS OF TUGHLUKĀBĀD.

[To face p. 76.

cities on either side; thus was made the fourth city, Jahānpanāh.

When Firoze Shāh had firmly seated himself on the throne, in succession to Mahomed Tughlak, he also constructed a city, Firozābād, four or five miles to the north-east of Siri, in 1354. The exact extent of this city is not quite certain, but it covered a portion of the modern city, and perhaps extended up to and round the Ridge, to the north.

After the Moghal conquest, Humāyun built the Purāna Kila in 1534. When he was turned out, Sher Shāh, or his son Islām, built the walls of a sixth city, which occupied a part only of Firozābād. Only a few hundred feet of the walls of this city remain, and even that short length is considered by some not to have belonged to the outer walls at all.

Finally, the seventh, and last, city was built in 1648 by Shāh Jahān, the third great Moghal emperor, who pulled down what was left of Firozābād, and of the walls of Sher Shāh's city, to build the walls of his own. No doubt the nobles followed suit, and quarried a great quantity of the stone walls for their own houses; but however that may be, the greater part of those walls have gone.

So we have traced, in chronological order, the

seven cities of Delhi. Now we come to the question, "What were the reasons which induced these monarchs to build new cities, instead of being content with the walls of the first, extended, if necessary, to contain a larger population?" To this, for answer, we may quote a native proverb, "Three things make a city—Dariā, Bādal, Bādshāh." That is to say, a river, rain-bringing clouds, or an emperor (who can enforce his wishes). Two of these three causes emphasize the necessity for water, without large quantities of which life in a hot country would soon become unendurable. The storage of rain-water in tanks may prove sufficient for ordinary purposes, but the river comes first in the estimation of the Hindu, because it is sacred, and in it he must bathe on festival days. All the great cities of Hindustān are situated on the banks of a river; Muttra, Kanāuj, Allāhābād, and Benāres are examples, which might easily be supplemented. It is, therefore, suggested that it was found necessary to move the cities of Delhi to the north-east, to follow the river, which once flowed not so very far from Old Delhi, but has gradually set further and further east—a process which is going on to-day, the extent of which has been considerable, even during the last century. In Daniell's "Oriental

Scenery," published in 1793, there is a plate, showing the river close up to the Kudsia Bāgh; now, even during the rainy season, it flows at a considerable distance.

The rivers of Northern India, in comparison with which the Thames is a mere rivulet, flow through plains of alluvial soil, and wander very considerably. It is often a matter of difficulty to keep them in their courses, and to prevent their leaving the large railway-bridges high and dry and finding a new course elsewhere; the soil is quite powerless to resist the cutting of the river, which is liable to sudden floods during the melting of the snows on the mountains and the heavy downpour of the periodical rains. In the cold weather, however, the volume of water is comparatively small, and the river is unwilling to give itself unnecessary trouble in cutting its banks, but follows a meandering course, loop following loop; it thus flows at a lesser velocity, and lives at peace with the banks. This condition of quiet is yearly disturbed. As the summer heats melt the snows, the river, which has been sluggishly flowing in its tortuous bed, begins to rise, and to spread itself over the spits, or spurs, which jut out at each bend; rising still further, it covers them entirely, and the channel becomes, it may be, a mile wide. Then come the rains, and a great flood comes down, invading a still greater area ; but this is probably covered with brushwood and vegetation, and the river is prevented from cutting away the soil, but encouraged to deposit its silt, so that, as the supply of melted snow and rain-water ceases, these lands are left by the subsiding river higher than they were before. In succeeding years, unless an exceptionally high flood should come down, the river will be less liable to cover these lands, and the general effect, therefore, of the annual rise of the river is to confine it within narrower limits, for the banks on either side are gradually raised. The Indus, however, not only raises its banks, but also raises its bed, and flows at a higher level than the surrounding country ; it has, therefore, to be confined for many miles between artificial banks, the duty of preserving which is one of the most unpleasant, which may fall to the lot of a canal engineer in Sind.

Now, while the river is in flood, it flows in a straight course and in short cuts across its loops. At the lower end of each short cut there is a sudden drop in the bed, and a greater velocity, the result of which is the erosion of the alluvial mud to such an extent that the projecting spur (now under water) may be cut right through, and the main channel of the river entirely altered.

The previous state of peace is brought to an end, there is a rapid in this part of the river, and the banks are cut away. The river, as it subsides, tries to resume a meandering course, but in order to do so has to change its course for miles above and below the rapid; rich fields may be swept away, the villagers may see their unripened crops disappear in the waters; their houses may follow suit; new lands may be left high and dry, which formerly were covered by the river, and in the abandoned bends are formed those "jheels," so well known to sportsmen. To use the words of Mr. F. J. E. Spring, C.I.E., an authority on this subject, "In the course of years there is scarcely an acre within the valley limits which will not, sooner or later, be eroded quite away, and in turn re-formed."

Shall we be very far wrong in assuming that this state of affairs existed in the Jumna valley, near Delhi, and that the liability of the plains to be flooded caused the founder of Old Delhi, whoever he may have been, to choose a site for his city on the rocky hills near the Kutb Minār? Is it not possible, even, that when Indraprastha was founded the river flowed about in its present course, and that gradually it took a more westerly course, encroached little by little, and swept the city away? Remember that the probable date of the foundation of that city was three thousand three hundred years ago: what changes cannot have occurred in that time? Nowadays the Jumna alters its course very slightly indeed: it is turned to the east by the fort of Salimgarh, and by the modern city, built on ground which centuries ago was at a much lower level, and not safe from flood. The extensive felling of Himālayan forests has caused a diminution of the precipitation of rain; the withdrawal of the greater part of its volume of water by great canals has rendered the river powerless. We cannot argue from the conditions of to-day in this river, but surely we can apply the results of observation of other rivers to imagine what once took place.

History and observation both suggest to us that the course of the river has altered within the last few centuries. Turkmān Shāh, the saint, is said to have lived and to have been buried on the banks of the river, and the Empress Riziyat was buried in 1240 on the river-bank. The graves of both are near the Turkmān Gate, far from the river, as it now flows. Mubārik Shāh, whose tomb has been mentioned, founded his incomplete city on the bank, and was buried within it. This tomb is not far from a ravine, which starts between the Ajmere and

Turkmān gates of the modern city, and looks extremely like an old bend of the river. Finch, who saw Delhi in January, 1611, calls this ravine, spanned by the "Bārah Palah" bridge, near Nizām-ud-din's shrine, an "arm of the Jumna." Then, again, the ravine which runs near the walls of the enclosure of Roshan Chirāgh Delhi, may be part of an old channel—a theory which is to some extent borne out by the fact that the walls of Old Delhi, where they cross the Kutb Road, appear to follow an old river-bank. In addition to this, we have a tradition that a Hindu king built the Kutb Minār in order to enable his daughter to daily see the river without the trouble of taking a fatiguing journey. This also may show that the river had receded. To show the effect of the canals on the river, it is on record that the reopening of the canal of Firoze Shāh, about 1820, caused the flood-level at Muttra to fall two feet. It is significant that the founding of Firozābād followed the first opening of that canal.

It may be objected that there is no absolute proof of all this, but as well might it be objected that the scientist is wrong, who attributes an incomplete skeleton to a certain antediluvian animal, because he finds two or three characteristic bones. A regular survey might throw more light on this question; but the processes of nature, slow but sure, have probably obliterated much of the evidence.

Whatever influence the "Dariā" had on the shifting of the cities of Delhi, there has certainly been a great change in the climatic conditions, so that the wells in Old Delhi have almost dried up, the tanks and reservoirs are never now filled, and it would be impossible for a large population to exist within the walls. The Hindu proverb thus is justified; and it was the vagaries of the river, and the failure of the clouds to pour down their waters, rather than the caprice of emperors, which have been the causes of the construction of so many cities, where one would have otherwise sufficed.

CHAPTER IV

OLD DELHI

The walls—Kutb Minār—Alāi Gate—Kuwwat-ul-Islām Mosque—Iron pillar—Tomb of Altamsh—Alāi Minār—Shrine of Kutb-ud-din—Jamāli Masjid—Tomb of Sultān Ghāri.

Map, p. 132.

THE walls of Old Delhi are twenty-eight to thirty feet in thickness, and about sixty feet in height above the ditch which surrounds them; the bastions are from sixty to a hundred feet in diameter; the intermediate towers are forty-five feet in diameter at the top, and well splayed out at the bottom. We are informed by Timur, in his Memoirs, that there used to be ten gates. From Adham Khān's tomb as a starting-point, near which is one of the smaller gates, the wall can easily be traced in a fair state of preservation, past the Ranjit (or Ghazni) Gate to the Fateh Burj at the corner, and thence to the Sohān Burj, where the high wall abruptly ends. A little beyond this was the Sohān Gate, and from about this point the ruins of a straight wall run across to Adham Khān's tomb. It has been contended, and it is probably the case, that these walls enclosed the citadel of Rāi Pithora, or Prithwi Rāja, the King of Delhi, who lost his life fighting against the Mahomedan invaders in 1192. We have reason to believe that the western wall was raised, and that outer defences were added to it, by the conquerors, who were determined that their foes should have greater difficulty in entering the city than they themselves had experienced. Alā-ud-din is known to have either strengthened the defences or to have built new walls about 1310; perhaps to him we may ascribe the construction of a further length of citadel wall, which was made from the Sohān Gate, across the Kutb Road, as far as the road to Tughlukābād; most of this section has now disappeared.

The outer wall of the city took off from the Fateh Burj of the citadel, and ran to a corner, afterwards joined to Siri by the wall of Jahānpanāh; thence the wall of Old Delhi ran east, crossed the road, and was continued to the corner, where the other wall of Jahānpanāh afterwards joined it. In this wall, which thus divided the two cities, were three gates; close to the junction was a postern leading to the Hāuz Rāni, now surrounded by a grove of trees. Between this postern and the road to Tughlukābād stood the Budāon Gate, from which, inwards, ran a street, which was the great bāzār, like the Chāndni Chouk of modern Delhi. In the plain, before this gate, many an unfortunate captive was trodden to death by elephants, or put to the sword, and piles of skulls were erected here. At this gate also justice was administered. A great reservoir was afterwards made on this side, some two miles long by one mile wide, and this was surrounded by pleasure-gardens; the water was probably held up by the wall of Jahānpanāh, which was made on an earthen embankment. The old wall extended for some distance beyond the Tughlukābād Road, and then turned to the Jamāli Masjid, and so back to the site of Adham Khān's tomb; in this section were the two remaining gates.

Outside the city, to the west, still stand the ruins of an Idgah; all round this, as is the case on the west of modern Delhi, were numerous graves of the Mahomedan inhabitants, and of those who were slain in the frequent battles and skirmishes on the plains to the north. Within the walls once stood many a palace, which has disappeared. We hear of the Kasr Safed (the White Palace, perhaps of marble), where Jalāl-ud-din ascended the throne, the Turquoise and

Green Palaces (which may have been behind the mosque), the Black Pavilion and the Red Palace, built by Balban. These were destroyed in the sack which followed the victory of Timur.

KUTB MINĀR.—Although this is sometimes supposed to have been built as the minaret of the mosque, close to which it stands, yet it is more probable that it is a monument of Victory, to record the Mahomedan conquest. It was started by Kutb-ud-din I-bak, while he was yet viceroy of Mahomed of Ghor, whose favourite slave and general he was, and after whose death he assumed the sovereignty of India, and was independent of Mahomed's successors. Shams-ud-din Altamsh, the slave and successor of Kutb-ud-din, completed the minār, and Alā-ud-din is said to have cased it in sandstone. Firoze Shāh repaired or rebuilt the two top stories, after the minār had been struck by lightning, in 1368, and it was probably he who introduced the marble. Lightning again struck and injured the minār in the reign of Sikandar Lodi, who restored it in 1503. After that time it does not seem to have received any attention until early in the nineteenth century, when it was in a terribly dilapidated condition as the result of earthquakes in 1782, and again in 1803. In 1828, Major Robert Smith, of the Bengal Engineers, was appointed to thoroughly repair this great monument, and spent seventeen thousand rupees in doing so, part of which sum was wasted in making the top ornament ; some five thousand rupees, in addition, were spent in the repair of the mosque and surrounding buildings. The work was well done, for an earthquake occurred in 1829, soon after the repairs were completed, but did no damage; the tower also successfully withstood the earthquake of 1905.

The top ornament, as designed by Major Smith, from the report of the villagers as to the original form, was an extraordinary structure. What remains of it is not so bad, but he put over the flat roof of the red sandstone pavilion a false dome of wood, and, surmounting this, a flagstaff, intended to fly the flag of the King of Delhi. This detail at once attracted the notice of the Governor-General, Lord William Bentinck, and he directed the wooden part to be taken down. The octagonal stone pavilion was removed, by the orders of Lord Hardinge, in 1848; it is understood that the Delhi jewellers had fashioned salt and pepper cruets in the shape of the restored minār, and had thus brought the open pavilion into some ridicule.

A great deal has been written in speculation

as to what the original form of the top of the minār was; there has been mention of a harp-like ornament, which one drawing seems to confirm, but this looks rather like a fanciful impression of the artist in water-colour. Major Smith, as we have seen, claimed that he had restored, rather than re-designed, the top. But it seems most probable (and a view in Daniell's "Oriental Scenery" confirms this) that there was a simple lantern and cupola, with four, or more, windows. The architecture of the period of Firoze Shāh, or that of Sikandar Lodi, does not suggest anything more ambitious than this, although it is not impossible that a pavilion of Hindu design surmounted the tower, when it was at first constructed. The memory of the oldest inhabitant, at the time of Major Smith's repairs, could not, however, have extended so far back as this.

The minār is some 238 feet high, 47 feet in diameter at the bottom, and 9 feet only at the top. It is divided into five stories by four balconies, the undersides of which are most beautifully carved in a design which recalls the "stalactite" stucco arches at the Alhambra in Granāda. The red sandstone balustrades were substituted by Major Smith for the battlements which once encircled each balcony. The first story is 95 feet high, with alternate semicircular and angular flutings; the second and third stories are 51 and 41 feet in height respectively, the flutings in the one being semicircular, in the other angular; while the last two stories are 25 and 22 feet high, and have no flutings at all. Round the tower are carved mouldings, containing the names and praises of the builder, Kutb-ud-din, and of his master, Mahomed of Ghor, with texts of the Korān and the ninety-nine names of Allāh, all written in the Kufic character.

The name may be derived from that of the founder, or the lofty tower may have been considered the "pole of the earth," or, again, it may have been called after the saint of that name, who lived and was buried near by. Such a magnificent monument has, of course, been claimed by the Hindus, as the work of one of their rājas. His daughter, it is said, was so pious, that each morning, before taking her food, she wished to go to the river to perform her ablutions, and, after the custom of Hindu ladies, to moisten with water her lucky neck-ornament, composed of nine different stones. But the journey became very tedious, and at last the rāja persuaded her to be content with a sight of the river, and therefore built this tower to enable her to do so. This tradition has been referred to in the previous chapter, as a possible indication of the receding of the river. Mr. Beglar, assistant to Sir A. Cunningham, contended that the minār really had a Hindu origin, declaring that only Hindus, with their proficiency in mathematics, could have designed such a structure; he sought to confirm his theory by working out a series of measurements, to which indeed many of the measurements of the minār conform rather closely. Moreover, the base of the minār is at the level of the foundations of the Hindu temple, which was afterwards altered into a mosque. Some of the moulded bands of stone round the minār have been deeply cut, which Mr. Beglar suggests was done after erasing some original carvings to which the Mahomedans objected. None of these arguments show that the Mahomedans did not employ Hindus to design and build the minār, which indeed they quite certainly did.

Sir A. Cunningham mentions some marks and an inscription on the south face of the plinth, indicating the plumb-line, but these have disappeared since his time, or, at least, have become very faint, and cannot be identified.

Alāi Darwāza, or Gate.—This was the work of Alā-ud-din Khilji, in 1310, and is the entrance gate to the mosque, as enlarged by that monarch: steps lead up from a ravine, which has

GATEWAY OF ALĀ-UD-DIN.

[To face p. 92.

become much silted up. In 1828 this gateway was in a sad state of decay, but it was then attended to, and the upper part of the exterior built up and plastered over; this naturally rather spoils the effect. The inside is as beautiful as ever, although some of the sandstone is flaking away with age. The diaper ornamentation ceases abruptly at the level of the commencement of the dome, but this leads the eye to notice the very effective pendentive arches by which the corners are spanned and the square building is brought to an octagonal shape: these arches are of a horseshoe form. At the angles of the octagon are brackets, which support the next course (which is circular) where it projects inwards, and thus the square is brought to a circle of a diameter of thirty-three feet. The walls are eleven feet in thickness.

Tomb of the Imām Zāmin.—It is interesting to notice what measures were adopted in forming the circular dome above this square building, which dates some two hundred and thirty years later than the Alai Gate. Here the octagon is formed by lintels across the corners of the main walls, and the outside of the dome, up to the cornice, is octagonal, instead of a circular dome starting from a square roof, as in the case of the gateway.

The octagon inside becomes a sixteen-sided figure in the next course, and brackets at the corners of this support the circle. This arrangement is rather a pleasing one. Other points of interest here are a western prayer-niche and the surrounding drip-stone, which is carved in the shape of prayer-carpets, arranged side by side—a compliment, perhaps, to the priest who is buried within.

The Imām Zāmin was Mahomed Ali Mashadi, vulgarly called Husāin "Pāi Minār," or Husāin who lived at the foot of the minār. He came here from Tous, in Persia, resided in Delhi for many years, and died in A.D. 1357.

Kuwwat-ul-Islām Mosque.—The meaning of this name is "The Might of Islām," fitting name for a mosque which was built by conquerors. It, quite certainly, occupies the same platform on which stood a Hindu temple, one of the twenty-seven which were despoiled by the Mahomedans of their pillars, to form the colonnades, and the mosque at the western end of the court; it is possible that the mosque was part of the original temple, but, otherwise, only the outer walls and the eastern steps were left in position. Carved bands run all around the platform, and the Iron Pillar rests on the original floor, overlaid by the Mahomedans with two thicknesses of stone in the

KUWAT-UL-ISLĀM MOSQUE.

[To face p. 95.

mosque and cloisters. For some unexplainable reason they laid three layers of stones in the court, which causes the drainage to run towards the cloisters—a most inconvenient arrangement.

The dome over the entrance, and the others in the colonnades, are quite different to the modern dome, which, if cut through the centre, would show bricks or cut stones, the sides of which point to a common centre. But here there is a different arrangement: each ring of stones has been placed horizontally over the top of that below it, and brought in a little in decreasing circles, the stability depending on the outer edge of the ring being adequately weighted. This idea is purely Hindu, for they did not know the principle of the ordinary arch until they were taught by their conquerors; but it is a very simple method of construction, and the top could be closed in with plain slabs. The outsides of these domes look like the ordinary dome, but this effect has been produced by building a false dome of masonry, shaped like a true dome on the outside only. These colonnades have been much admired, and justly so, but the credit for them belongs rather to the Hindus than to the Mahomedans, who merely rearranged the pillars and roofs. The pillars are well carved, although not in such relief as those on Mount Abu. The figures have been much damaged by the bigoted Mahomedans, but the conventionalized leopards' heads show to what ideas of art the Hindus had attained in the eleventh century (if not earlier): there is a little picture of a cow licking her calf, while it drags at her udders, most faithful to life.

Iron Pillar.—The exact age of this marvellous monument is a matter for considerable speculation, but there is an inscription on it in a language not now in use, which was current between the third and sixth centuries of the Christian eras. This inscription records the erection of the pillar (but not the place or date of doing so) by a king, whose name is read Chandra, or Dhāva, by differing authorities, who, however, agree that he was a votary of Vishnu. It is rather curious that this Vaishnavite king flourished here, not ninety miles from Muttra, then a stronghold of Buddhism; but Buddha taught reverence to Brahmins, so that toleration was the order of those days. To Mr. James Prinsep is due the credit of deciphering this ancient inscription. There is also inscribed on the pillar the record of the building, or rebuilding, of Delhi by Ang Pāl, in A.D. 1052, and some five later inscriptions of little interest.

It is a mystery how the Hindus were able

to make this heavy pillar, of a metal the purity of which must be great, or it would surely have rusted almost away in all these centuries. There is no deposit of iron ore in the neighbourhood; even had there been, how did they manage the forging of this great mass? It seems a wild conjecture to suggest that it may have been a meteorite; but even so, an immense amount of patient work must have been necessary before it assumed its present shape.

Mayo Arch.—There is a point of interest about this arch, and those on either side, which formed the facade of the mosque. The courses are horizontal, and the arch is formed by shaping the inner edges of each course; but the back of the arch shows that the idea of the true arch had begun to be explained to the Hindu masons, for some of the stones are cut so as to take a certain amount of thrust. The great ruin of these arches is probably due to their instability, although the gradual disintegration of the stone has been, no doubt, a contributory cause. The central arch is forty-three feet high.

Tomb of Altamsh.—It is unfortunate that this has no roof, for then some idea could have been formed as to how far Hindu masons had progressed in forty years under the tuition of

Mahomedan architects. But the pendentive arches at the corners are of the "horizontal" type, so that it seems unlikely that a dome could have been successfully attempted. The square has, however, been brought to the circle, and several circular stones have been put in place; some have argued from this that a dome once crowned it. Altamsh died in 1236, and troublous times followed, which may have been the cause of the work having been abandoned; had there been a dome, its fall would have injured the cenotaph of the king, which does not appear to have sustained any damage.

A close study of the interior decoration and architecture of this exquisite mausoleum will, at every step, cause renewed admiration at the whole conception of the work, the skill, and the resource of the long-forgotten architect. The exterior is quite plain, and the walls are seven and a half feet in thickness.

Alāi Minār.—To the north of the tomb of Altamsh are the remains of piers intended to support arches, in continuation of those previously built; the second unfinished minār was to have been the companion to the Kutb Minār, but of double the diameter, and high in proportion. The ruins of it are only so far interesting as to show how the latter was constructed.

SHRINE OF KUTB-UD-DIN BAKHTIĀR KĀKI.—This, as already stated, is situated in the village of Mahrāuli. The saint, commonly called the Kutb Sāhib, came from Ush to Delhi very soon after the conquest of this place by his namesake, the general of Mahomed of Ghor; here he lived, near the Jamāli Masjid, for over half a century, and died in A.D. 1256, in the reign of Altamsh, who is said himself to have performed the funeral ceremonies. Yet his shrine remained comparatively neglected, until one Khalil-ulla Khān built an enclosure wall in 1541. We may suppose that his sanctity preserved his grave intact against marauders and the Mewātis, then Hindu, who occupy the country to the south. The name "Kāki" was given to him because he was supposed to live on small cakes of that name, which fell, like manna of old, from heaven.

The enclosure lies at the foot of the hill, on which is the "Jumping Well," and is entered by a gate, after the passing of which there appears, on the right, a long marble screen, practically hiding the shrine; this was the gift of the emperor, if he may be so styled, Farukhsiyar, in the early part of the seventeenth century. On the left is the back of the mosque of the saint, with the grave of an unimportant individual at the corner. In an adjoining court, in which there is a bāoli, or open well, there are two graves of some little interest, near the steps leading down to the well. One of these is that of Zabitā Khān, a Rohilla Pathān; the other is reputed to be that of his son, Ghulām Kādir, who put out the eyes of the unfortunate Shāh Alam; but it does not seem likely that this is so. There is only one more grave to notice about here, that of "Dāi-ji," presumably somebody's foster-mother.

On the left of the entrance-gate, as one emerges, there lies the tomb of Mohtamid Khān, historian of Aurangzeb, separated from the enclosure-wall of the shrine by a path; to the left of this path is the entrance to the Moti Masjid, a mosque of no particular interest, built in 1709. Beyond this mosque is an enclosure, in which are buried three of the later Moghal kings—Akbar Shāh II., Shāh Ālam, and Shāh Ālam Bahādur Shāh, the successor of Aurangzeb. Between the graves of the two last is a space, which was destined for the body of Bahādur Shāh, who lies far away in Rangoon. And this exhausts all that is of any interest. Possibly some of the nameless graves contain the bones of brave men who fell on the plains, towards Safdar Jang's tomb, either in the first conquest by Kutb-ud-din, or when Timur defeated Mahomed Shāh, or in repelling invaders from the north at other times.

Close by this group of buildings is the family cemetery of the nawābs of Jhajjar, the last of whom was hanged for complicity in the Mutiny of 1857; his body was disposed of as that of a common felon, and is not here.

JAMĀLI MASJID.—This mosque is said to have been built on the platform of the dwelling of the saint Kutb-ud-din, and the whole village is said to be as old as the fort of Rāi Pithora. The mosque was attached to the tomb of Shaikh Fazl-ulla, or Jalāl Khān, a celebrated poet, who wrote under the *nom-de-plume* of Jamāli, and died in A.D. 1535. His mausoleum, once his dwelling-place, is well built, with tile ornamentation, and has two verses of the poet inscribed within.

TOMB OF SULTĀN GHĀRI.—Some three miles to the west of Old Delhi, in Mālikpur (now within the limits of Māhipālpur), is the tomb of Abul-Fateh Mahomed, son of Altamsh, who died in Bengal in A.D. 1229. The term "Sultān Ghāri," given to the tomb by the common people, means the "Cave King." It is a curious octagonal structure, sunk in the middle of a raised courtyard, so that the roof is attained by a few steps only. It is possible that a second story once existed, which may have been covered by a "horizontal" dome, such as those in the Kutb Mosque. Some authorities consider the building to have been Hindu; if so, it is curious that a Mahomedan should have been buried within it. Close by are the tombs of Rukn-ud-din Firoz and of Muiz-ud-din Bahrām Shāh, sons and successors of Altamsh; Firoze Shāh records the repairing of these three tombs, the domes over the two latter having fallen

CHAPTER V

SIRI, TUGHLUKĀBĀD, AND JAHĀNPANĀH

Foundation of the three cities—Tughlukābād—Tomb of Tughlak Shāh—The city—Khirki Mosque in Jahānpanāh—Sāt Palah—Tombs near Khirki—Roshan Chirāgh Delhi—Bedi Mandal—Begampur—Shrine of Khwāja Nizām-ud-din Auliā—Adjacent buildings.

Map of Tughlukābād, p. 104.

SIRI was built by Alā-ud-din in A.D. 1303. The site of this city is partially occupied by the village of Shāhpur, but hardly anything of the walls remains, for they were removed by Sher Shāh, to build the walls of his city. We know from the Memoirs of Timur that there were seven gates, of which three opened towards Jahānpanāh, but we have mention in history of the name of only one, the Bāghdād Gate, presumably one of those on the western side. The walls, we are told by Ibn Batuta, were seventeen feet in thickness, but only mounds of earth remain to mark their position. Inside this city there was a Palace of a Thousand Pillars, but this also has gone, and the only monument connected with the city which now exists is the Hāuz Khās of Alā-ud-din, seldom visited, and worthy of no special mention.

Tughlukābād was founded by Tughlak Shāh about A.D. 1321, and must have been constructed with great rapidity, for that monarch only lived until 1325, and no work can have been done after his death. The plan shows the walls and gates: what authority, other than tradition, the compilers had for the names of the gates is not known.

The walls of Jahānpanāh were constructed, about A.D. 1328, by Mahomed Tughlak: there were six gates in the western wall, and seven in the eastern, but the name of one only survives, the Maidān Gate on the west, near an old idgāh. The walls of this city also were removed by Sher Shāh.

TUGHLUKĀBĀD.—This city may be approached from three sides: there is a road from the Kutb Minār; there is another from the railway-station of Tughlukābād; and there is a rough track, unmetalled and unbridged and badly maintained, which approaches the city from the small station of Okhla. The middle course is the best, but also the longest and hardest to arrange; by it,

THE CITY OF TUGHLUKĀBĀD.

To face p. 104.

however, can be seen two forts which lie to the south of the city. The nearer was built by Mahomed Tughlak, and called the "City of the Just Man," an attribute to which he did not add that of "merciful." It is also called by his name.

TOMB OF TUGHLAK SHĀH.—This lies about midway in the south-western side of the city, and opposite the citadel. It is built in a fortified enclosure, which was once surrounded by water, held up by a dam, thrown across the valley near Mahomedābād Fort. The Tartar was always careful to build his tomb during his lifetime, for he could never be sure of any one performing that office for him after his death; Tughlak had already built one tomb for himself in Multān. His habitual caution is shown by the fortification of a tomb built in a lake, but it is probable that he used this little fort as a summer house, and did not wish to be surprised outside the walls of his citadel.

The approach is by a causeway, under which the water has long ceased to ripple, and the openings in which have become silted up. The entrance to the enclosure is by a fine gateway, commanded by a bastion close by, and, even if the gate were forced, it would not be easy to get in alive, for there is a sharp turn, and the steps are open to attack from above. The masonry is magnificent, the stones with which the fort is built are very massive, and many must weigh five tons apiece; the walls slope from the top, and the whole effect is one of stern grandeur.

The interior of the fortified enclosure is raised, and is probably built above an outcrop of rock, or this may have been arranged to provide the height for the underground apartments. The shape of this fort is singularly irregular, and flanking defence was fully provided, by corner bastions. The parapet is raised, and the embrasures are rather curious, three upright stones forming two openings for fire, with a curved stone across the top to protect the head. One other feature in the surrounding walls must be noticed: Hindu pillars, lintels, and slabs are introduced in places, and thus break the monotony of the arcades below the parapet.

In the arcade to the left of the entrance there is a small grave, which is reputed to contain the bones of the favourite dog of Tughlak Shāh; this is a wonderful tribute to that animal, when we remember that dogs are considered unclean by Mahomedans. On the south side of the work there is a place for drawing up water from a shallow well sunk in the rock below. At the western corner of the pentagonal fort there have been preparations made for a tomb; this was to have been similar to one at the other corner, which contains the bones of a great minister of Tughlak Shāh, and is crowned by a marble dome. The underground apartments are approached from the arcades.

The king's tomb (see p. 193) is within the enclosure, is massive and plain, but yet effective, with panels and a band of marble to break the monotony of the red sides. The marble facing of the dome was probably the first to be attempted, and is therefore not particularly well fitted. The chief feature of the exterior is the tremendous "batter," or slope of the walls, a feature which is absent in the earlier tomb of Altamsh, or the Alāi Gateway, but is characteristic of buildings of this period. Its introduction may have been due to experience of earthquakes. These walls are over eleven feet in thickness at the base and only four feet thick at the top. The interior is plain. Above the pendentives to the dome, which are generally similar to those of the Alāi Gate, are lozenge-shaped stones instead of brackets to support the upper course of the development of the circle, thirty-four feet in diameter.

There are three graves inside—those of the founder, his wife, and son Mahomed ibn Tughlak: in the grave of the latter were placed a number of deeds of acquittance, as mentioned in the history, on page 197.

THE CITY.—A detailed examination of the ruins of the walls would take too long, but attention may be drawn to a few prominent objects which have escaped destruction. The citadel is entered by a small postern-gate at the head of a winding approach from the causeway. This postern is in a fair way to fall down, but, while it stands, it shows a very fine arched roof with well-cut stones; there is no sign of a hinge to any door. Within this gate there is a reservoir, half filled with the débris of the old walls, yearly, for want of a little attention, subsiding under the effects of tropical rain. Somewhere beyond this reservoir there was the palace, while to the right of a rising footpath there is the inner citadel, part of the wall of which serves as the side of another great reservoir. The gate of this inner work has fallen, a huge column lies underfoot, and within all is ruin and confusion. At the side of the reservoir last mentioned there rises a ruined building with underground passages, once stables, or rooms for retainers, now the haunt of leopard or skulking jackal. From the top the eagle eye of old Tughlak Shāh must have often fallen on the Kutb Minār, away to the west.

KHIRKI MOSQUE.

To face p. 109.

It is sad indeed to see these Cyclopean walls rent asunder by pipal trees (the seeds of which have found shelter in the crevices), disintegrated by rain and wind, and fast being levelled with the dust. It may not be out of place to express a hope that the efforts of restorers may be directed to this city, founded so carefully on the solid rock, and deserving a better fate. Restoration will never make it habitable, on account of the want of water; so that there is no fear of incurring the wrath of the saint who cursed it. It would be most interesting to see the citadel of this fourteenth-century city as it was; this is not impossible of attainment, for the stones have not been removed to any great extent.

Khirki Mosque.—The village of Khirki lies just within the south-eastern wall of Jahānpanāh, and the mosque is a very fine one. It was erected about A.D. 1380. In plan it is square, and within the encircling wall there is a colonnade; but the interior, instead of being left open, as other mosques of the time were, has arcades in the shape of a cross: four open courts are thus left. The roofs are supported by massive monolithic columns, which are the feature of mosque architecture of the period, but they are differently disposed. At each corner of the four open courts four columns are grouped together, and along the sides of the courts there are double columns, while the roofs of the surrounding arcades are supported, sometimes by single, sometimes by double columns, but all symmetrically arranged; the illustration gives a very good idea of the arrangement. The small sections thus formed are covered in by low vaults, but at each intersection of the arcades there are groups of nine domes rising from the flat roof; there being nine such intersections, there are eighty-one domes, and the total is made up to eighty-five by the addition of four domes, one over each of the three entrance-gateways and the fourth over the prayer-niche to the west. The gateways and prayer-niche are flanked by sloping towers, similar to those at the Kalān Mosque. The windows in the outer walls are closed by heavy sandstone grilles. Hindu architecture is represented by heavy door lintels, and by the drip-stones around the courts supported by lintels on brackets, also shown in the illustration. Altogether this mosque is well worthy of an inspection.

Sāt Palah.—In the wall of Jahānpanāh to the east of the village of Khirki there is a double-storied "regulator," of seven openings in each tier, through which were drawn off, from time to time, the waters of the lake, which was held up

SATI MONUMENTS NEAR TUGHLUKĀBĀD.

MOSQUE AND TOMB OF YUSUF KATĀL.

[To face p. 111.

by the wall. The date of the erection of this was A.D. 1326, in the reign of Mahomed, son of Tughlak Shāh.

Tomb of Shaikh Yusuf Katāl, disciple of Kāzi Jalāl-ud-din, Lahori.—This lies just north of the village of Khirki, and dates from somewhere about A.D. 1500. It is a pretty little pavilion with a small dome supported by twelve pillars, which are filled in between by pierced red sandstone screens. It may have been taken as a pattern for the tomb of the Imām Zāmin, near the Alāi Gate, under the Kutb Minār. The drip-stones are carved to represent tiles, and encaustic tiling brightens the cornice round the dome. A ruined little mosque stands close by. From here a good view is obtained of the walled enclosure of Roshan Chirāgh Delhi.

Tomb of Kabir-ud-din Auliā.—This building, of red sandstone, with marble decoration and sloping walls, resembles the tomb of Tughlak Shah; it stands a little to the north-west of the last-described building, and contains the remains of the son of Yusuf Katāl. It is called the "Lāl Gumbaz," or red dome.

Not far off, there is a small object which looks like a chance rearrangement of some stone pillars which had been found lying about;

on the top is a stone, shaped somewhat like the half of a pumpkin. Below ground is a tiny cell, only three feet wide, and almost filled up with soil. This is declared to have been the abode, below by day, and above by night, of Kabir-ud-din Auliā, who is buried in the Lāl Gumbaz; but one may be pardoned for being sceptical about this. Hard by there is a well, which bears the date of A.D. 1410.

To the north and east of this may be traced the ruins of the walls of Siri, and trees, half hidden, to the north, mark the village of Shāhpur. The wall of Jahānpanāh ran outside the enclosure of Roshan Chirāgh Delhi.

Tomb of Bahlol Lodi.—About half a mile to the eastward of the tomb of Kabir-ud-din Auliā there is a mausoleum, built in the same style as that of Yusuf Katāl; close to this is the rather roughly built tomb of the first of the Lodi dynasty. It has twelve doors, and five domes, and was probably the summer-house of the king during his lifetime. The garden round it has long since ceased to bloom, but water to irrigate it in abundance must once have flowed in the deep and sandy ravine, on the farther bank of which is the enclosure of Roshan Chirāgh Delhi. Bābar, in his Memoirs, mentions having visited the garden. Around the mausoleum there is now an extensive cemetery.

ROSHAN CHIRĀGH DELHI.—This was the name given to one Nasir-ud-din Mahomed, disciple of Shaikh Nizām-ud-din Auliā, and successor of that saint; he died in 1356, his shrine was built by Firoze Shāh in 1373, and the enclosure-wall was added by Mahomed Shāh in 1729. The shrine resembles that of his master, and requires no description; it is not worth inspection.

BEGAMPUR MASJID.—A cross-country path skirts the village of Begampur, which contains two mosques, the larger of which takes its name from the village, and was built about the same time as those at Khirki and in Firozābād. Both mosques have numerous domes on the vaulted roofs. In the village there is also the Kalu Sarāi, which has been much knocked about.

BEDI MANDAL.—The use of this building, which is close to Begampur on the west, cannot be exactly stated. It consists of a small room, with sloping exterior walls, on a high mound, which was once faced with masonry, and was built, most probably, in the reign of Mahomed Tughlak; Hindus, however, consider that it has a much greater antiquity. It may have been used as a watch-tower, or have formed part of the Palace of a Thousand Pillars; or, again, it may have been the building into the foundation of which many Moghal skulls were built, and have been a tower of Victory. But this is only speculation, and its original use will probably never be known.

SHRINE OF KHWĀJA NIZĀM-UD-DIN AULIĀ.—This group of buildings belongs to the time when Siri and Tughlukābād were being built, and is in the environs of the former, so will be described here.

In 1303 a great horde of Moghals, under Tarma Shirin, invested Delhi for some months, but suddenly broke up their camp, and retired. It was supposed that this was due to the efficacy of the prayers of this saint. He was the disciple of one Farid-ud-din, who was a disciple of Kutb-ud-din, who, in his turn, was the disciple of the famous saint of Ajmere, Muin-ud-din; his claim to saintliness was, therefore, a strong one. In these days, he is considered the greatest of them all. His differences with Tughlak Shāh have already been mentioned; when Nizām-ud-din heard that the king was coming to chastise him, he calmly said, "Dilli hinoz dur ast" ("Delhi is yet a long way off")—words which have become a proverb, for Tughlak never reached Delhi. General Sleeman, the great authority on the Thugs and principal exterminator of that garotting sect, mentions, as a significant fact, that Thugs, both Hindu and Mahomedan, worshipped at this shrine; but then they were peculiarly superstitious, and this may have meant little, although it is more than probable that Nizām-ud-din plotted against Tughlak Shāh, and had a hand in his death. The descendants of the sister of Khwāja Nizām-ud-din are guardians of the shrine to this day, and are at all times exceedingly courteous; the father sheltered a number of European refugees from massacre in Delhi in 1857.

The shrine, as it is to-day, has been embellished by gifts from many generous Mahomedan kings and nobles. The date of the death of the saint is given on the front of the Jamāt-khāna Mosque close by, as A.D. 1325. This mosque was built by Firoze Shāh in 1353; the centre dome of the five is no less than fifty-two feet in diameter, by far the biggest dome of that period.

Jahānārā Begam.—This princess is one of the attractive personages of Indian history. She was a firm supporter of her eldest brother,

Dāra Shikoh—certainly a more attractive character than "that nimāzi" ("that bigot"), as he called his brother Aurangzeb, who put him to death. Jahānārā shared the captivity of her old deposed father until his death, and then came to Delhi, was received with favour by her brother, the Emperor Aurangzeb, lived here fifteen years, and died in 1681.

The full text of the inscription on her headstone runs as follows :—

> "Except (with) grass and green things let not my tomb be covered ; for grass is all-sufficient pall for the graves of the poor. The fakir, the transitory one, Jahānārā Begam, disciple of the saintly family of Chisti, daughter of Shāhjahān, may God illumine his intentions."

It will be remembered that the Emperor Akbar regarded Salim Chisti of Sikri with great respect, even naming his eldest son after him. Salim Chisti also was a spiritual descendant of Muin-ud-din of Ajmere.

TOMB OF SHAMS-UD-DIN MAHOMED, GHAZNĀVI, TAGA KHĀN, AZAM KHĀN.—When Humāyun was defeated at Kanāuj, by Sher Khān, he escaped across the Ganges, but would have been drowned had not a soldier extended a hand to him and saved him ; that soldier was the noble who here lies buried. He accompanied Humāyun throughout his wanderings, and his wife was one of the foster-mothers of Akbar; consequently that emperor held him in high esteem. Akbar appointed Shams-ud-din Chancellor of the Empire; after the latter was murdered by Adham Khān, in a manner to be related, Akbar continued his favour to the sons and relatives of this noble, who were known, by the jealous, as the "tribe of foster-brothers."

The mausoleum is decorated, both outside and in, with plaster and mosaic, and the floor is laid with black-and-white marble stars; marble appears in much of the other decoration, and the dome is overlaid with the same material. There are three graves within, those of Shams-ud-din, his wife, and his brother; the mausoleum was erected by his son, Mirzā Aziz Kokaltāsh, who built the Hall of Sixty-four Pillars close by.

CHAPTER VI

FIROZĀBĀD AND THE DELHI OF SHER SHĀH

Extent of Firozābād—Sher Shah's walls—Kalān Masjid—Kotila of Firoze Shāh—Asoka Pillar—Jāma Masjid of Firoze Shāh—Kushk Anwar—Purāna Kila—Kila Kona Mosque—Tomb of Mahomed Shāh—Buildings in Khairpur—Jantar Mantar—Kadam Sharif—Old Idgāh.

THE limits of the city of Firozābād are extremely difficult to trace, because the city of Shāhjahānābād was built at such a short distance, as to make it easier for the inhabitants to pillage the building materials of the older city than to obtain them from further afield. A part of the older city was included within the newer, but the greater part was abandoned.

Roughly speaking, the city extended over a semicircle, with a radius of a mile and a half from the centre of the Kotila on the river-bank. Starting from this point, the edge of the houses ran along Dariāganj, and then across to the end of the Chāndni Chouk. The line of the houses then ran along the Chāndni Chouk, to about where the Lahore Gate was afterwards built; there could hardly have been houses to the north of this street, for most of that part is open, even to this day. The limiting line then trended south, between the Kadam Sharif and the later walls. This part of the city was probably rather sparsely inhabited, up to the great ravine; beyond that there was a thickly populated portion, which lay between the present city walls and the Purāna Kila. But round the Ridge there was a considerable suburb, adjoining the hunting-park of the emperor, which was surrounded by a high wall, of which no trace remains.

Tradition says that the channel through the Faiz Bāzār formed a part of the canal of Firoze Shāh, which he made to bring water into Delhi, but its further course we cannot trace. The canal of Ali Mardān Khān, which has been frequently mentioned, was a later one, and an extension of Firoze Shāh's canal to Hissar.

It seems probable that the city of Firoze Shāh had no walls; on the riverside, outside the Kotila, there was no necessity for one, and Shāh Jahān did not build a wall on that side of his later city in 1648. The remains of the "Khuni Darwāza," in the Chāndni Chouk, may perhaps indicate an old gate, but this is very doubtful.

On the southern side, the great ravine would make a continuous wall difficult to build, and, had one existed, we should expect to find the upper part of this ravine filled up, which is not the case. So we may consider Firozābād to have been a collection of suburbs, with no containing wall, Firoze Shāh having only concerned himself to build a wall round his Kotila and round his hunting-park. Had there been the materials for a wall, it is not likely that Sher Shāh would have despoiled Siri and Jahānpanāh of their walls, in order to surround his city and raise the walls of the Purāna Kila. Again, it does not seem to have been a matter of difficulty to occupy Firozābād; fighting frequently took place in the streets; kings, when they were threatened, preferred to shut themselves up in Siri; when Timur came, it was the old cities of Siri, Jahānpanāh, and Delhi which were held against him. All this goes to show that Firozābād was not a walled city.

If we accept the fact that Firozābād had no city walls, we can quite understand why Sher Shāh should wish to build defensive walls. He chose that portion of Firozābād which lay contiguous to the Purāna Kila; but how much of his walls he was able to complete is very doubtful, for his reign was a short one. His son

Islām was not much at Delhi during his troublous reign, but the work commenced by his father may have steadily proceeded, in spite of the attention devoted to the new fort of Salimgarh. On the whole, however, we may suppose that the city wall was never completed. As designed, the city was probably intended to have the Kotila of Firoze Shāh at the north-eastern corner, and the Purāna Kila at the south-eastern corner; if houses then extended as far as Humāyun's tomb, they would have been left in an unprotected suburb, for the walls standing opposite the Purāna Kila must be part of the city wall. The only cause for doubting this fact is the statement of William Finch, who visited Delhi in 1611, about seventy years after the building of Sher Shāh's city, and forty years before the walls of Shāhjahānābād were started. He says, distinctly enough, "The city is two kos between gate and gate, begirt with a strong wall, but much ruinate." Further, he says, "About two kos without Delhi is the remainder of an ancient mole (mahal), or hunting-house, built by Sultan Berusa (Firoze)." This makes the distance from the Ridge to (say) Humāyun's tomb four kos, or eight miles, whereas it is only six miles; but his idea of a kos is very hazy. He makes eighty-one kos from Agra to Delhi Shershāhi, a distance of less than a hundred and twenty miles. If we take his kos as being a mile and a half, we have to place the south gate at the Arab Sarāi, near Humāyun's tomb, the north being the solitary gateway, which is near the jail. It is hard, however, to understand how he could miscount the number of kos, when each kos was marked by a prominent pillar, most of which are standing to this day; if the "kos minārs" were really erected by Jahāngir (as that king says), at a later date, we can easily account for it, because the natives reckon a kos rather by time taken than by actual distance, and he probably got his information from native retainers. The point is not, perhaps, one of great importance; it only shows the difficulties of reconciling such information as we possess of those times with the monuments we have remaining to us to-day.

Kalān Masjid.—This mosque stands near the Turkmān Gate, within the walls of the modern city, but was also included within the limits of Firozābād; the word "kalān" means "great," but the word has been corrupted, and the building is sometimes called the "Black" Mosque. The style is the same as that of the Khirki Mosque, built at about the same time, 1380, but has a single open court; the sloping

KALĀN MASJID

[To face p. 122.

exterior of the walls, the tapering towers, the massive columns of quartzite, the rough nature of the arches, the stones of which are not dressed to fit, but depend for their stability on the strength of the mortar—all these points are characteristic of the period. Hindu architecture also had its influence, for stone lintels are common, and the drip-stones are supported by lintels on brackets. There are fifteen low domes over the mosque proper, arranged in three rows, and the same number cover the arcades—all are true horseshoe arches, which were prevalent before the bulbous dome came into fashion in the time of Shāhjahān.

Kotila of Firoze Shāh.—The surrounding walls of this have been removed, in order to provide materials for the walls of the new city, but a few fragments still stand here and there; the masonry is of a very rough type, and the local quartzite is used. The rooms must have been dark and inconvenient; the vaulted roofs depend on the mortar for their strength.

The buildings within the castle have fallen into ruin, and it is difficult to trace the uses to which they were put; a few still stand, noteworthy among which are the building on which was set up the Pillar of Asokā; the Jāma

Masjid; a circular building with a number of underground rooms; and some ruins which are supposed to have comprised the emperor's palace. There is a tradition that underground passages extend from this citadel to the Ridge, and also to Old Delhi, but this is improbable. That one ran along the riverside through the palace is not so unlikely, but exploration would be extremely unpleasant, not to say dangerous, for the passage must be infested with snakes.

PILLAR OF ASOKA. — There is a drawing extant, which shows the building on which this is set up faced with red sandstone, but this may be imaginary. Formerly there was a black-and-white pavilion surrounding the pillar, which was surmounted by a golden ball and by a spire of the same metal; these were in place in 1613.

The inscriptions of Asoka on the pillar are in four compartments, at the four cardinal points, and also around the lower part. They are edicts, couched in rather egotistic language, and were given in the twenty-seventh year of his reign, after his conversion to Buddhism; they cancel other edicts issued in the twelfth year of his reign. He calls himself Devānampiya Piyadāsi, each of which names means "beloved of the gods," and urges the priests to convert all, including even his own queens and women. He also records the planting of trees on all roads, the digging of wells at every mile, and the erection of sarāis, for the benefit of travellers. Curiously enough, many subsequent kings take to themselves the credit for similar acts.

Jāma Masjid.—This stands close to the pillar, and is said to have been connected to the building on which the latter stands by a bridge. The unevenness of the ground caused the builders of the mosque to make a lower story beneath the mosque. The gateway is on the north side, for the river was then so close that an entrance from the eastern side was difficult; access was also given by staircases from the lower story.

Timur was much struck by the beauty of this mosque when he saw it in 1398, twenty years after it was built. He carried away with him a number of masons, and erected afterwards, in Samarcand, a mosque which was adapted from the design of this one. It had four hundred and eighty pillars of hewn stone, with vaulted roofs, and at each corner there was a lofty minaret; the doors were of brass, and the walls and domes were decorated with inscriptions, including the eighteenth chapter of the Korān.

We may presume that this mosque was of similar design, and Captain Francklin, who saw this mosque in 1793, bears this out. He describes it as having four cloisters, the domed roofs of which were supported by two hundred and sixty stone columns, each about sixteen feet high. There was an octangular dome of brick and stone in the centre of the mosque, and about twenty-five feet high. One account calls this the "Marble Mosque," but very little of that material can have been employed.

Hardly three walls of the building remain entire; the pillars have been removed, and there is strong suspicion that some were built into the bastions of modern Delhi by British engineers. The sandstone grilles which filled the window-openings have also gone, and but the shell of a fine building remains.

Kushk Anwar, or Mehndiān.—Across the road, on a rising ground, and near the jail, there stood a palace of Firoze Shāh, of this name. It is probably this group of buildings which is depicted in one of the plates of Daniell's "Oriental Scenery." There was a central building, with a many-roomed lower story, and above this a domed pavilion, with twelve monolithic pillars; at the four corners of the main building, but

KILA KONA MOSQUE.

[To face p. 127.

separated from it, there were towers of peculiar shape, like the little paper towers (Mehndiān) which are made on the occasion of a certain festival. These towers had, on the top, little pavilions, each consisting of four pillars, lintels, and a pyramidal roof.

PURĀNA KILA, OR INDARPAT.—The Hindu tradition of the antiquity of this fort has been disposed of. It was founded by Humāyun, in 1534, but the walls were built of stone and mud, and the son of Sher Shāh, Islām, pulled them down soon afterwards, to rebuild them in lime. Only the main gate is used now, there being a tradition that the northern gate was closed by some king, who ordered it to be shut behind him as he went out to battle, and never to be reopened unless he returned victorious.

KILA KONA MOSQUE.—There is no date on this mosque, but it is agreed that it is the work of Sher Shāh; it must have been built about 1541. It differs from any built before it, and is much more ornate. It has three-storied corner-towers at the back, which is not, as in former mosques, left plain, but the ugly area of bare wall is broken by an ornamented band of tiling and by some balconies, also decorated with tiles. On either side of the projecting "kiblah-gāh," moreover, there are sloping towers of the style of the period of Firoze Shāh. On the front of the mosque there is exceedingly effective decoration, containing such features as engrailed arches (like those at the Alāi Gateway), Hindu drip-stones supported by brackets, and a combination of black and white stone, "sang mousa," and "sang marmar." The interior presents a variety in the corbelled pendentives, which is repeated in the great mosque of Akbar at Fatehpur Sikri. Altogether, this mosque shows a great advance in architecture, and yet we can trace the influence of earlier styles in attaining such a pleasing result. The mosque has only one dome remaining out of three.

Tomb of Mahomed Shāh.—Close to the road which runs from Humāyun's tomb to Safdar Jang's tomb, and not far from the village of Khairpur, stands a tomb which attracted the attention and admiration of Fergusson, the writer of a standard work on architecture. It contains the remains of the third king of the Sāyyad dynasty, who died in 1445. The shape is octagonal, with an exterior arcade, the columns of which contain massive grey monoliths, such as are characteristic of the period of Firoze Shāh.

The columns, which are at the angles of the arcade, are buttressed, and the "pendentives" of the small domes above the arcade are similar to those in the tomb of Altamsh and in the Alāi Gateway. Round the interior of the main dome there is a cornice, decorated in a manner which indicates the style of the former decoration of the whole of the interior of the mausoleum.

GATEWAY AND MOSQUE OF KHAIRPUR.—A few hundred yards from the tomb of Mahomed Shāh, in the village of Khairpur, there stands a building with a lofty dome. This is generally supposed to have been the entrance to the adjoining mosque, although there is another entrance which has been closed up. It may have been a mausoleum, but there is now no grave within it. The dome is an extremely fine one; the walls of the building are not buttressed, as one might have expected in a building erected at the beginning of the sixteenth century. The exterior of the doorways is decorated with black and red stone, after the fashion which was afterwards adopted for the gateway of the Purāna Kila. The interior is dark and stern, and impressive; the pendentives, although similar to those of the Alāi Gate, are formed as true arches, and niches above give to the dome its great height.

Lastly, the heavy lintels and brackets, some of which are very fine, show the influence of the earlier Hindu style.

The mosque is of massive masonry, with the buttresses and sloping corner-towers, which are characteristic of earlier times. The plaster decoration on the arches, and inside, is picked out with paint; an inscription announces the building of the mosque in the time of Sikandar Lodi, about A.D. 1500.

TOMB OF IBRĀHIM LODI.—Close to the mosque there stands the tomb of this monarch, who lost his life in 1526 while attempting to stem the tide of the Moghal conquest. It is distinguished by encaustic tilework, the use of which had not long come in; and there is a prayer-niche, a feature which was dying out. From the northern window may be obtained a view of the tomb of Sikandar Lodi; this is in a walled enclosure on the banks of a ravine, which lends it additional height and an imposing appearance. Sikandar's Tomb combines most of the features of the adjacent buildings, with the addition of some enamel work on the arches and on the fillings of masonry over the doors. Close by there is a bridge of seven arches, which spans a ravine, and carried the high-road from the north, or gave an approach to the gardens of Sikandar Lodi, which were about here.

Jantar Mantar.—The buildings which comprise this observatory have already been noticed, but a few further details may be given. The group strictly belongs to Shāhjahānābād, but stands in the environs of Firozābād. Maharāja Jāi Singh erected a number of these observatories, others being situated at Muttra, Benāres, Ujjāin, and Jāipur, the city which he built to replace Amber. After comparing the results, which were obtained from observations taken at all these places, astronomical tables were constructed, which excelled in accuracy any then known, and are used in India to this day by numerous astrologers. So anxious was the Maharāja to obtain real accuracy that he rejected instruments of brass, made after the pattern of some in Samarkand, because he found the wear of the bearings to be excessive.

Kadam Sharif.—The interpretation of this name is the "sacred footprint;" there is here a slab of stone, which is supposed to bear the imprint of the foot of Mahomed, for which reason it is also known as the "Kadam Rasul," or foot of the prophet. What it is like, exactly, cannot be stated, for the slab is contained in a basin of water, on the surface of which float rose-leaves. The basin is constructed over the grave of Fateh Khān, son of Firoze Shāh, and associated with him as joint monarch; he died in 1374, and was here buried by his heart-broken father, who placed over the tomb the sacred stone, which had been sent by the Imām of Mecca.

The enclosure surrounding the tomb stands to the west of, and at some considerable distance from, the road, which runs from Old Delhi, to the end of the Sadr Bāzār, on the west of the railway. The path to the enclosure is bordered, on either side, by thousands of graves, both old and modern, for this is the Mahomedan cemetery of modern Delhi, and all desire to rest as close as possible to the sacred slab.

The tomb itself stands in a court, which is surrounded by colonnades; the sloping roofs of these are supported by pillars in the Hindu style, while the domes are the pointed ones of the period. The covering to the grave has similar pillars, but at each corner there is a kiosk, and the central dome is a peculiar one. Opposite the steps, which lead up to the raised platform of the enclosure, is the grave of Shams-ud-din, Nawāb of Firozpur, hanged for participation in the murder of Mr. William Fraser in 1835.

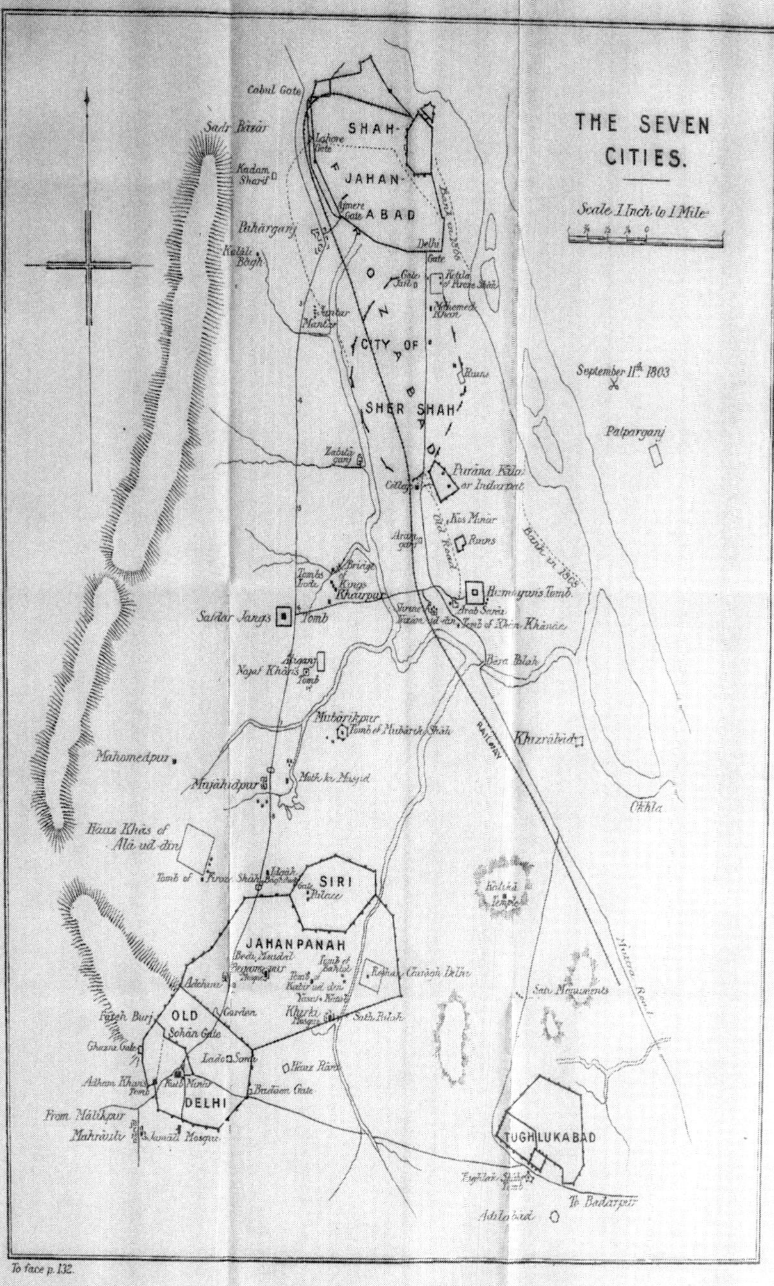
THE SEVEN CITIES.
Scale 1 Inch to 1 Mile
SHAH-JAHAN-ABAD
Cabul Gate
Sadr Bazar
Lahore Gate
Kadam Sharif
Ajmere Gate
Paharganj
Delhi Gate
Kalali Bagh
Jail
Kotila of Firoze Shah
Jantar Mantar
CITY OF SHER SHAH
Ruins
September 11th 1803
Patparganj
Purana Kala or Indarpat
College
Kos Minar
Old Road
Bank in 1803
Ruins
Bridge of Kings
Tombs
Kharpur
Humayun's Tomb
Safdar Jang's Tomb
Arab Sarai
Tomb of Khan Khanan
Bara Palah
Najaf Khan's Tomb
Mubarikpur
Tomb of Mubarik Shah
RAILWAY
Khizrabad
Mahomedpur
Moth ki Masjid
Majahidpur
Chhla
Hauz Khas of Ala ud-din
Tomb of Firoz Shah
SIRI
Palace
Kalika Temple
JAHANPANAH
Chiragh Delhi
Muttra Road
Sath Monuments
Fateh Burj
OLD DELHI
Sohan Gate
Garden
Khirki Masjid
Sath Palah
Ghazni Gate
Lado Sarai
Hauz Rani
Adham Khan's Tomb
Kutb Minar
Badaon Gate
From Malikpur
Mahrauli
Jamali Mosque
TUGHLUKABAD
Tughlak Shah's Tomb
To Badarpur
Adilabad

To face p. 132.

OLD IDGĀH.—At the back of the Kadam Sharif enclosure, on the rising ground which forms the continuation of the Ridge, stands the Idgāh. This is the place of worship to which Mahomedans repair on the two great festivals, called Id; the one follows the fast of Ramzān, the other celebrates the intended sacrifice by Abraham of Ishmael (not of Isaac, as we are told). This Idgāh is within a fortified enclosure, made to protect the worshippers while at their prayers, for in the fourteenth century people were not above attacking their praying enemies.

CHAPTER VII

SHĀHJAHĀNĀBĀD

The walls—St. James's Church—Adjoining houses—Magazine—Old cemetery—Nigambodh Gate—Salimgarh—Garden of Mādho Dās—The Palace before 1857—Courts and buildings—Dariāganj—Jāma Masjid—Objects north of the Ridge—Coronation Darbār Park—Badli-ki-Sarāi—Garden of Mahaldār Khān—Roshanāra Garden—Mithāi bridge—Hindu Rāo's house.

Map of Delhi in 1857, *p.* 172.
Plan of the Palace, p. 160.

THE walls, built in the time of Shāh Jahān, about A.D. 1648, did not completely surround the city, which was left open on the river side. A portion of wall, however, was constructed from the Water Bastion to about opposite the Government College, more as a protection to the adjacent houses against the river than as a defence against an enemy. The river-face of Dāra Shikoh's palace (afterwards the arsenal) also had a protecting wall. It was not until after 1804 that the city wall was extended, in the bed of the river up to the moat around the palace;

the wall along Dariāganj was probably built at the same time. That no wall was originally made along the riverside we know from the writings of Bernier, the French physician, in 1669, and of Captain Francklin, who visited Delhi in 1793.

The line of the walls, as first constructed, was broken at intervals by round towers, one of which has again been exposed by the removal of the Garstin Bastion; there was a musketry parapet, but no cannon were mounted. The improvement of the defences was undertaken soon after the Mahratta siege of 1804, and the bastions, then constructed, received the names of prominent men of the time, such as Moira, Burn, Garstin, Ochterlony, and Wellesley. The work must have been spread over several years. A ditch with a glacis was made; many houses were removed, which nestled close up to the walls and prevented a clear field of fire; and Martello towers were constructed, which were separated from the main walls by a drawbridge, and intended to fire into the city in case of a riot.

The Nigambodh and Kela Ghāt Gates were built at this time. The Calcutta Gate was not built until 1852, when the Grand Trunk Road was brought through the Chāndni Chouk; this gate was removed, within fifteen years, to admit the East Indian Railway. The Cashmere Gate was built about 1835; the Lahore Gate (since removed) was made a double gate in 1852. The other gates, except the Mori Gate, remain as they were.

St. James's Church.—This was commenced in 1826, and took ten years to build, at a cost of ninety thousand rupees, provided by the munificence of Colonel James Skinner, C.B., whose descendants also have done much to improve the structure. The design is due to two officers of the Bengal Engineers. Major Robert Smith built it up to the cornice of the entablature (or top of the columns), while Captain De Bude completed the work. The dome was much damaged by shell-fire during the siege, and at least one shot went through the dome; but it was restored by 1865, and the iron rails supporting the roof were presumably then built in. There is some legend about the number of shot-holes piercing the copper ball and cross which were taken down from the top after 1857, but the actual number seems to coincide with no number of any significance.

To the west in the churchyard is the grave of Mr. Fraser, who was shot on the Ridge in 1835. The tombstone was erected by his friend, Colonel

Skinner, and was of marble, surmounted by two lions, with an iron railing round; all that remains is the inscription, but possibly some of the marble columns, scattered about the place in confusion, once adorned the tomb. The destruction must have taken place in 1857. Just behind the grave is a marble cross, to the memory of several Europeans who were massacred, and whose bodies were found lying here. In the north-east corner is the grave of Sir Thomas Theophilus Metcalfe, Bart., B.C.S., the father of Sir John Theophilus Metcalfe, who was the joint magistrate of Delhi in 1857, and had a narrow escape.

ADJOINING HOUSES.—The houses along the river-wall at the back of the church are, perhaps, a hundred years old. That nearest the Civil Courts was known in 1845 as the house of "Smith Sāhib;" it was probably occupied by a Mr. George Henry Smith, who was collector of customs, north-west frontier. It has an extensive range of underground apartments. In the house next to St. James's Bastion there was published, in 1857, the *Delhi Gazette*, the editor of which was a Mr. Place, and the sub-editor a Mr. Wagentreiber; here also was issued the *Delhi Sketch-book, or Indian Punch.* The open ground in front of this house used to be laid out as the gardens of the Residency, which in 1857 had been converted into the Government College. The house which is nearest to the Cashmere Gate was, in 1857, occupied by a Major Fuller, Director of Public Instruction, an appointment then open to officers of the Company's army.

Colonel Skinner's house was afterwards the Bank of Bengal; it has now been acquired by the East Indian Railway, which is rapidly taking up many houses in this quarter of the city, and therefore the history of these houses may well be placed on record. Behind what is now St. Stephen's College there lay the house of Ahmad Ali Khān, which has been converted into a number of small dwellings, but was occupied after the siege for some time as barracks; there are still to be seen traces of the European soldiers' tendency to scribble on the walls. Opposite here the road once took a considerable bend to avoid a house, described in 1845 as that of the Company's chief judge, but occupied in 1857 by the head master of the Government College, Mr. Roberts.

MAGAZINE, or ARSENAL.—This is said to have been formed on the site of the palace of Dāra Shikoh, eldest son of Shāh Jāhan; the office of the executive engineer, Provincial works, may have formed part of this palace. Certain underground passages, discovered some years ago, but now closed up again, indicate the existence of the usual "ty-khāna," or underground apartments. The city wall here is at some distance from the river-wall of the palace, at the back of the post-office enclosure. The outside of the city wall is furnished with stakes, projecting downwards, while older portions, towards the Water Bastion, are without them. Moreover, old blocks of grey stone taken from dismantled buildings are built into the base here; these also indicate the later date of this portion of the wall.

At one time a very considerable quantity of powder, shot, and shell was collected here, as well as the largest siege-train in all Northern India; but Sir Charles Napier, when Commander-in-Chief, objected strongly to the proximity of these large stores to the palace, and to their location in the heart of the city, far from cantonments. The greater part of the powder and cartridges was therefore removed to a new magazine near the Ridge; but a certain amount of powder was kept here to be made up into cartridges, and sent from time to time to replenish the other magazine. The guns also were left here, and thus the rebels, in 1857, easily became possessed of a train of guns, heavier than any the besiegers could bring against them. The present post-office building was the armoury. An old powder-magazine stands close by, and the guns were parked on the ground where the telegraph-office now stands. Behind were two small magazines, which were blown up by the gallant little band of defenders, as will be elsewhere related. Round the walls, which have now, except for a small portion, been removed, were "lean-to" sheds, containing various stores; the arsenal office was where the office of the executive engineer now is. Across the road, then paved with cobble-stones, and on which no one was allowed to smoke, were the workshops, the two gates of which faced the gates of the arsenal enclosure. The houses at the back of the workshops have been swept away by the railway.

Old Cemetery.—This lies under the south wall of the enclosure; most of the graves are nameless, and an inscription on the cross in the centre of the cemetery records that this was the case in 1857 also. An exception is a grave under a canopy, which bears an inscription to say that it was erected by Colonel Skinner to the memory of one Thomas Dunn; another grave is that of a young son of Lieutenant Raynor, one of the brave defenders of the arsenal close by.

Nigambodh Gate.—Close to this gate there used to be some flour-mills, driven by the canal of Ali Mardān Khān, but these mills have fallen into ruin, for steam is now the order of the day. Through the gate the corpses of Hindus are borne to the burning-ground in the river-bed beyond. The Nigambodh Ghāt lies outside the gate, but the tradition of great antiquity which is attached to it has been disposed of; the ground, right up to and beyond the railway-bridge, lies too low to have escaped flooding. The site of the Calcutta Gate is not far off, and is recorded on a small railway-bridge.

Salimgarh.—This old fort was built by Islām Shāh in 1646; it is called the "fort of Salim," the name by which he was usually known. It was built on an outcrop of rock, and the river then flowed east of it, but afterwards set in and filled the channel between Salimgarh and the mainland. Jahāngir built a bridge to span this channel; part of this bridge afterwards joined the fort of Shāh Jahān to Salimgarh, but it has been removed for the railway. The places where it abutted on the walls may still be seen. The Grand Trunk Road bridge, close by, was built in

1852, after which date the bridge of boats, previously established opposite the Rājghāt Gate, was brought up to about the line of the railway-bridge, which was completed about 1864. The railway now runs through Salimgarh, and a portion of Shāh Jahān's Castle has been cut off to make room for it. Little now remains of any of the buildings in Salimgarh, which was once used as a state prison: it was much damaged by the fire of our guns, from a battery established in the Government College gardens after the assault.

Bagicha, or Garden, of Mādho Dās.—This is situated close to a bridge, which carries the canal over the road leading up from the Nigambodh Gate to the Chāndni Chouk. There are here temples to Sacha Narāyan, Badrināth, and Rādha Krishnā, all of which are titles of Vishnu, or of his incarnations. On the last-named temple is some curious work in glass, made to look like mother-of-pearl. Here also is the place where Mādho Dās was buried (not burnt), for this is the custom in the case of ascetics, who are of no caste; even Brahmins have their sacred string removed and burnt after their initiation.

The Palace.—In the first chapter some account was given of the interior of the Fort, as it is now styled, and of the buildings as they exist to-day, in a more or less mutilated condition, in spite of liberal restoration by the British Government. It will, however, be interesting to attempt to reconstruct the palace, as it existed in the days of Aurangzeb, with the later additions to it, up to the time of the Mutiny, after which such destruction was perpetrated, in order to find room for the unlovely barracks.

In our endeavour to do so we shall be aided by the writings of Bernier and Tavernier, who visited Delhi in the seventeenth century, and by those of Sāyyad Ahmad Khān, who wrote in 1847. The map opposite page 160 is taken from a plan by a native artist, which is in the records of the India Office; this appears, from internal evidence, to have been drawn about the same time, at all events before 1852.

The magnificent lofty battlemented walls were carried round the city side of the castle to three-storied towers at the north and south ends of the river-face. Between these the wall was made lower, and along a terrace, formed at the level of the top, were the principal residences of the emperor and his ladies, thus assuring a good view of the river, and every chance of cool nights; the days could be spent in underground apartments behind the thickness of the wall. On the city side of the castle there is a deep moat, once kept filled with water, and stocked with fish; since 1857 no water has been allowed to stand in the moat. A glacis also has been formed, and has extinguished the green gardens which lined the moat and contrasted with the rose-red walls. The gates of the castle are the Lahore and Delhi Gates, the Water Gate (at the south-east corner), a small postern about the centre of the river-face, and the Salimgarh Gate, which opened on to the bridge leading into that fort. The moat was spanned by wooden drawbridges, and the present stone bridges were not constructed until 1811—a fact which is recorded by an inscription over the gate leading into the barbican, in front of the Lahore Gate. This barbican, with the one in front of the Delhi Gate, was made by Aurangzeb, who objected to the clear view into the palace which the people could formerly obtain, whenever the gates were opened.

In front of the Lahore Gate there was a great square, in which those Hindu nobles, whose turn it was to mount guard, encamped during their twenty-four hours of duty, for they never cared to trust themselves within the walls. To the south of this square there was constructed the "Ellenborough Tank," about 1846. This tank, being of red sandstone, was called the "Lāl Diggi," and was about five hundred feet long by a hundred and fifty feet wide, with towers at the four corners, and steps at the two ends; it was filled with water which flowed into it through the Chāndni Chouk. It has now been filled in with earth.

Within the Lahore Gate is a vaulted, covered arcade, with rooms on either side, and an octagonal open court half way, called the "Chatr Chouk," or Umbrella Court; from this steps lead to the top of the Lahore Gate. On these steps the Commissioner of Delhi was cut down on the fateful 11th of May, 1857. The rooms over the gate were made by closing in the arches of the once open pavilions with brickwork.

Court of the Nakkār Khāna.—The covered passage mentioned gave access to a square court, surrounded by arcades, in which were sheltered the troops of the Mahomedan nobles when on guard. From this square, to the right, and through a gateway with three doors (now removed), there runs a straight road to the Delhi Gate, with a canal down the centre. On either side of this road there used to be a raised footway to keep the foot-passengers safe from the crowded traffic. Bordering these footways there were lines of double-storied houses, with gates, at intervals, giving entrance to the quarters for the nobles and the various workshops on the west side, and to the Mina Bāzār and servants' quarters on the east. The line of this road was continued through a corresponding triple gate on the north side of the Nakkār Khāna court along the Salimgarh Road. This road was bordered by other quarters, and the stables lay beyond a third triple gate, near which there ran the canal, which entered by way of a bastion, at the angle of the castle, close by here. In the court of the Nakkār Khāna, or music-gallery, the nobles had to alight from their elephants, and enter the next court on foot. Over the dividing gateway were stationed the musicians, with their hautboys, cymbals, serpents, and other strange instruments, and the enormous drums, which announced the arrival of the emperor to take his seat on the throne in the Diwān Ām.

Court of the Diwān Ām.—This also was surrounded by arcades of a single story, and was of magnificent dimensions, a hundred and eighty yards wide by a hundred and forty yards long. The arcades were apportioned to the different nobles, who vied with each other in their decoration, so that rich carpets, velvets, and silks were disposed in profusion. Between the gateway and the Diwān Ām there seems to have once been a terrace, about a hundred yards long and ten wide, on which there stood an enclosure, with sandstone screens around, called the "Gulāl-bāri." This term, however, was also given to the private enclosures of the emperor, and it may have referred to the balustrade which surrounded, at a little distance, the Diwān Ām, and outside which the courtiers of lower rank had to stop, unless summoned within it.

The Hall of Public Audience stands opposite the gateway; the sixty pillars were once covered with polished limewash, with paintings and gilded flowers such as still adorn the Diwān Khās. The emperor sat on his raised throne, attendants standing beside him with peacock fans and flaps to drive away the flies; below the throne sat the prime minister on a marble seat; he alone spoke to the emperor, and transmitted the petitions. The pillars of the hall were hung with brocades; satin canopies concealed the roof; silk carpets were spread on the floor; and, on three sides of the hall, there was pitched a gorgeous red tent supported by silver-plated poles, and lined with flowered chintz. Round the raised throne, at a little distance, there was a balustrade covered with gold or silver plate, as the importance of the occasion demanded, and outside this railing the great nobles stood, their eyes downcast and their hands folded. A marble balustrade filled in the spaces between the outer pillars of the hall, and on this were beautiful gilded vases; the courtiers of lesser degree were stationed outside this and under the tent. While the emperor was seated on his throne, musicians played soft music, which did not disturb but pleased the ears. At the back of the hall, in a raised gallery, the band was stationed at other times to fill the courts behind with sweet music.

When the business of hearing petitions, or of presenting ambassadors, was finished, elephants, horses, antelope, rhinoceros, panthers, and a number of other animals or birds were brought in for the emperor's inspection, or the cavalry might be reviewed, and the young soldiers called on to try their strength at sheep-cutting. On some days the emperor attended the chief court, which was situated in a corner of the square, and himself took a seat on the bench to hear the cases.

Justice then was rough, without coded laws, and very ready. The malefactor did not linger in prison, but was speedily removed, to be crushed to death by an elephant, or otherwise executed; sometimes he was condemned to be bitten by poisonous snakes.

On either side of the court of the Diwān

Ām there were gateways which led, that on the right to the domestics' quarters, that on the left to the store-rooms where various state appurtenances were kept, and to the imperial kitchens. To the left of the hall, in the east wall of the court, there was yet another gate, which opened into a small court; out of this other gates led, one to the Regalia Chambers, another, always covered by a red curtain, to the court of the Hall of Private Audience.

Court of the Diwān Khās.—On three sides of this court also there used to be arcades; on the fourth side was the terrace, on which the lovely Hall of Private Audience is situated, close up to the river-wall. This terrace used to be screened on the river side by pierced marble screens; a low marble balustrade extended along the inner side, which was shut in by cloth walls. Round three sides of this hall also was stretched an awning, which was fastened to the pavilions at either end of the terrace, and supported on the third side by poles overlaid with gold plates.

The privilege of entering this court was only accorded to those high officers of state with whom the emperor was wont to consult, or to ambassadors and other persons of rank who were invited to the honour of a personal interview. To the left hand of a person entering the Lāl Pardah Gate, and in the corner of the court, was the Pearl Mosque with its three gilded domes; this was separated from the baths by a narrow alley, which led through a gate into the Hyāt Baksh Garden.

Diwān Khās.—All the palace buildings on the river-terrace were of the same general plan as that of this hall; a description of it will therefore apply to the others, except that they were not so elaborately decorated. In plan the hall is oblong, with a central room, surrounded by a colonnade or verandah. The roof of the central room is supported by twelve pillars, forming three openings on each of the four sides; the room is therefore "bārahdari," or twelve-doored. The roof of the outer verandah is at the same level as that of the central room, and is supported by twenty pillars, so that there are thirty-two pillars in all. These are not all of the same shape; those at the corners and along the longer sides are more massive than the others. The intervals between the pillars are spanned by scolloped arches, a feature of Moghal architecture in Delhi. The spans of the roofs are reduced by marble slabs curved inwards, and the roofs themselves are of wooden planks, carved and painted;

formerly these were overlaid with silver plates. The pillars and walls above are covered with gold painting and inlaid work of precious stones. Above the end arches on both of the short sides of the central room is inscribed the famous couplet—

> Agar fardos ba rue zamin ast
> Hamin ast o hamin ast o hamin ast.

The hall is open on three sides, but some of the openings towards the river have been filled in with glass windows; this was probably done comparatively recently. The openings on the other three sides were closed by hangings, which were replaced by scented grass screens in the hot season; awnings were spread on these sides. The floor was covered with rich Persian carpets; underneath flowed water in a marble channel, covered over with marble slabs.

There is no decoration on the exterior of the hall, which is of plain marble, but the surface is broken by recessed panels. On the four corners of the roof are small marble "chattris," or small umbrellas; these are little pavilions, each with four slender pillars and a dome. Marble domes have replaced the original ones, which were of fluted copper plates, overlaid with thin sheets of gold.

Hammām.—Close by the main entrance from the terrace into the baths there is a small chamber containing a bath, let into the ground, and said to be made out of one block; the small size suggests that it was the bath set apart for the children. On the ceiling, now covered with whitewash, were, it is said, pictures of animals, to frighten naughty children. A passage, parallel to the river-wall, traverses the building, and to the right of this is a bath-chamber, used during the hot weather; in the further recess of this is a shower-bath. In the centre of the larger chamber of this cool room is a shallow basin, ornamented with jade, a small piece of which yet remains. It is a custom among Hindu women to wear a necklace, composed of nine different stones, with a jade pendant, as a charm; each morning this is washed with water, and the water is drunk to avert sickness, or the charm may be merely sucked. This idea is said to have suggested the ornamentation of this basin, but the precious stones have, of course, long disappeared. These charms are called "nau-rattan," and curios composed of nine different stones are frequently offered for sale by the Delhi jewellers to-day.

To the left of the main passage there are two more chambers, the first of which is a cool room, which, however, could be heated if so desired; warm water could be admitted to flow in the channel which surrounds this chamber, and which is paved with mosaic, so arranged that the flowing water should seem to contain fish. In the side room of this chamber there is a marble couch, on which the coffee and hookah could be enjoyed after the bath had been taken. The walls are beautifully ornamented with mosaic up to the level of a man's waist, and the upper part is supposed to have been painted, but the pictures have been covered with whitewash for many years.

The next room was the hot room, warmed by fires under the floor; the fuel was introduced through holes in the floor of a passage, which is at the end nearest the Pearl Mosque. It is said that four tons of wood were necessary to heat up the baths.

Moti Mahal.—The main passage through the baths has been blocked at the north end, through which one could formerly pass on to the river-terrace again; it is now necessary to make a detour. On this part of the terrace there once stood the Pearl Palace (the term "Mahal" really means "Seraglio," but may, for convenience, be rendered "palace"). Between the baths and the site of this palace Bahādur Shāh erected, about 1844, the Hirā or Diamond Mahal, a small irregular pavilion; the water-channel in front of this was furnished with a number of fountains, and the edges were gracefully curved.

The Pearl Palace was of red sandstone, but was covered with polished whitewash (or else faced with marble), painted and gilded after the fashion of the Diwān Khās; it had five pierced windows towards the river. Above were two balconies, from which the emperor and his ladies could watch, secluded from the public gaze, the elephant combats, or troops passing in review, on the river-bed below. The hall was removed after the Mutiny, because it prevented the free circulation of air to the barracks, but why a portion of the unimportant Hirā Mahal was left instead one cannot understand. On the garden side of the hall there used to be a marble bath, about twelve feet square and five deep, with four legs, all carved out of a single block of marble; it was brought from Makrāna, in the Jodhpur State.

North of the Moti Mahal a small pavilion abuts on the three-storied Shāh Burj, and beyond, in the corner of the castle, there used to be the Jahāngir Garden and the quarters allotted to the princes and their families.

Hyāt Baksh, or Life-giving, Garden.—This large garden was at the back of the Moti Mahal, and was about five hundred feet square; it was bounded, on the one side, by the baths, the Pearl Mosque, and a wall, continued in line with these two buildings; on the other by a wall, running from the Shāh Burj. Outside this wall there ran the canal, and against the wall was a pavilion, still standing, built of marble, with a marble basin surrounded by shelving slabs. The water, entering from the canal at the back, flowed over these slabs in sheets, and thus represented the rain as it is wont to fall in the month of Bhādon, or August. In a corresponding pavilion, against the opposite wall, there is no basin, but a channel, into which the water fell in a smaller stream, as the rain falls in Sāwan, or September; this water was probably filled into reservoirs at the top of the pavilion by hand, for it could not be well fed from the canal. In the marble basin of the Bhādon Pavilion there are recesses, in which camphor candles were placed, giving a beautiful effect as the water fell in front of them; similar recesses are fashioned behind the cataracts in which the water escaped. Each pavilion had four gilded turrets.

In the centre of the garden, and of a reservoir, there is a building made by Bahādur Shāh in

1842, and called the "Palace of Victory" (*sic*), or the Water Palace; it has since been used as a bath for the British soldiers of the garrison. At the corner of the reservoir there stood a tree, called "pakal" (*Ficus venosa*), which was milked twice a day; the milk was esteemed for its medicinal qualities.

Mahtāb, or Moon, Garden.—This lay between the Hyāt Baksh Garden and the Salimgarh Road; the water from the canal in that road entered by a cascade. To the south of this garden was the Chobi Mosque, built by Ahmad Shāh, presumably for the use of the attendants; there were also buildings of utilitarian purpose, such as the stores and the kitchens.

Khās Mahal.—Having dealt with the buildings to the north of the Diwān Khās, which has already been noticed on page 150, let us proceed along the river-terrace to the south of that building. The group next to it contains the dwelling-place of the emperor, his sleeping apartment, and an octagonal tower, Musamman Burj, out of which projects a balcony. This is comparatively modern, as the following translation of the inscription will show; it starts in the north-east corner, and reads—

"All praise and worship be to God, the Lord of the world, who made this emperor the king of kings, who is the son of kings, and of Timur's royal line; he is the protector of the world, who holds his court in heavenly places, with a starry host; the upholder of religion, the father of victory, the great furtherer of the faith, the lord and conqueror of the world of his age, the shadow of God. On the face of the Musamman Burj he raised a new seat, such that the sun and moon, beholding it, are ashamed. The poet laureate was ordered to find a chronogram, so that it might remain in black and white, and the Sāyyad devised the following: May this remain the seat of Akbar Shāh, of ancient lineage, A.H. 1223."

The last sentence, reckoning the value of the Arabic letters according to what is called the "Abjad," gives the year after the Hegira, or flight from Mecca, of Mahomed in A.D. 622; the date corresponds to A.D. 1810, the Mahomedan year being lunar. The whole is a very flowery description of Akbar Shāh II., a monarch, who was dependent for his safety and income on the Honourable East India Company.

On the inner wall of the room which is immediately behind the balcony is a fine inscription, which runs—

"O thou, whose feet are fettered, and heart closed, beware!
O thou, whose eyes are closed, and feet set fast in mire, awake!

O thou, who goest west, with face turned east, looking back, mind thy goal!"

A text, no doubt, for the eyes of the emperor as he rose in the morning. Over this room there is now a marble dome, which has replaced one of copper-gilt; this was sold by auction after 1857.

The part of the Khās Mahal through which flowed the water-channel was called the "Large Sitting-place;" on the inside of the arch, which spans the channel, above the beautiful marble screen, there are four verses, of which the lower to the right reads—

"The Lord of the world, founder of this heavenly building, Shāhab-ud-din Mahomed, the second to be born in a most prosperous hour, Shāh Jahān Bādshāh Ghāzi, opened the door of bounty to the peoples of the world."

Rang Mahal.—This apartment lies to the south of the Khās Mahal, and has been considerably defaced, by having been turned to use as an officers' mess-room. It was formerly surrounded by a garden-court, called the Imtiāz Mahal, or Palace of Pre-eminence. All around this court were arcades of red sandstone, surmounted by some two thousand gilded turrets.

MARBLE SCREEN.

[To face p. 158.

North and south, in the centre of the garden-walls, were pavilions of marble, similar to those in the Hyāt Baksh Garden. In the centre of the court was a basin, as much as a hundred and fifty feet square, fed by the stream which flowed along the terrace; there were twenty-five jets of water in the open channel leading to the reservoir. At either end of the hall there projected into the garden a kiosk, and under one of these was the entrance to the underground apartments.

In the centre of the entrance-hall of the Rang Mahal there was a representation of a lotus-flower, over the leaves of which the water bubbled and fell into a shallow marble basin; this was inlaid with mosaics, representing rose-petals and jasmine-blossoms, which seemed to move as the water swirled over them. The water escaped over the edge of this basin, and flowed, in a cataract, into the garden below. The roof of the Rang Mahal was once of silver, but in the days of Farukhsiyar copper was substituted for the silver; later, Akbar II. replaced the copper by a wooden ceiling, painted vermilion. The hall has seven windows towards the river.

At the south end of the terrace in the Imtiāz Mahal was a small pavilion, corresponding to the one in the Khās Mahal, and called the "Small

Sitting-place." Between this and the Rang Mahal there was a high marble screen, to shut the women in from the view of dangerous lovers; similar screens were placed in between all the buildings to the south; they were carved with scolloped recesses.

Dariā, or River, Mahal.—Next came a small and comparatively modern apartment, with two openings towards the river; this stood in a narrow court, fitted in between the Imtiāz Mahal and the next large court. It was much more ornate than the others, and had a pediment, on the river-face, surmounted by the figure of a bird. The building was probably made of ordinary materials, and has been removed.

Mumtāz, or Little Rang Mahal. — This building still stands, and is in the same style as that of the Rang Mahal; it was used by the princesses for their dwelling. It has five openings towards the river, and once had the usual garden with running water, fountains, and marble basins, on the edge of which the ladies sat and embroidered little hand-bags, in which they carried sweets and betel.

Khurd Jahān.—Last of the seraglio buildings on the river-face, there came the "Little World,"

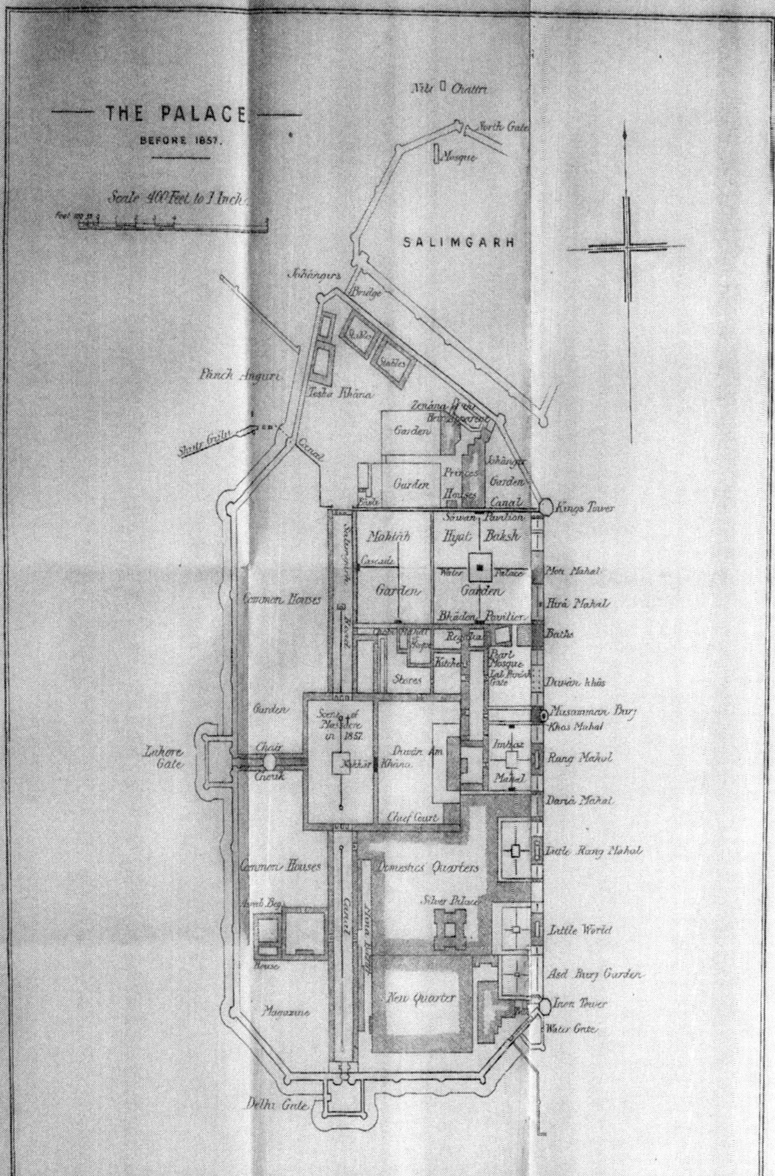
THE PALACE
BEFORE 1857.
Scale 400 Feet to 1 Inch
Nili Chattri
North Gate
Mosque
SALIMGARH
Jehangirs
Bridge
Stables
Panch Anguri
Tosha Khana
Zenana Gate
Garden
Garden
Princes Houses
Jehangir Garden
Canal
Kings Tower
Hyat Baksh
Mahtab
Cascade
Garden
Garden
Water Palace
Moti Mahal
Hira Mahal
Baths
Pearl Mosque
Stores
Kitchen
Diwan khas
Musamman Burj
Khas Mahal
Common Houses
Garden
Lahore Gate
Chouk
Diwan Am
Imtiaz Mahal
Rang Mahal
Daria Mahal
Chief Court
Little Rang Mahal
Common Houses
Domestics Quarters
Silver Palace
Canal
Little World
Asd Burj Garden
New Quarter
Iron Tower
Water Gate
Magazine
Delhi Gate

To face p. 160.

Why it was so called we do not know, unless within it there were collected different flowers and trees, and all that was necessary to make it like the world on a small scale. What a pity that all has gone! the delightful walks, the shady kiosks, the fountains, the grottoes, the lofty terraces, carefully watered, on which the ladies slept in the sweltering hot nights. Yet some may object that it is better so; that the vast sums necessary to keep up all this magnificence were ill-spent. We must remember, however, that these sums were distributed among many thousands who worked at the embroideries, the paintings, the dresses (so fine that a single night's wear would destroy some), and that the arts and craft of Indian workmen have suffered by the want of demand for such work. Gladly would the people of Delhi see the old days back again, and money flowing like water.

The part of the castle, which lies between the apartments last mentioned and the road to the Delhi Gate, was filled with quarters for the domestics of a humble nature; but there appears to have been amongst these a "Silver Palace," of which we know nothing, for it has been swept away. There was also another garden close to the rive r-wall and to the three-storied "Lion Tower," which had an adjoining pavilion like that at the Shāh Burj. Near this were some underground baths.

DARIĀGANJ.—From the little Golden Mosque, which stands outside the Delhi Gate of the palace, a road runs through the Fāiz Bāzār to the Delhi Gate of the city. On the east of this road there was, in 1857, a dāk bungalow, and to the west of it stood a great mosque, the Akbarabādi Masjid, built by one of the wives of Shāh Jahān. This mosque was swept away to give a clear field of fire from the fort.

From the Golden Mosque there runs a road to the Rājghāt Gate also. About half way to the gate, there now stands a cross marking the site of the old Baptist Chapel and of the native Christian cemetery, which surrounded the chapel. The road beyond this point used to be in a cutting, but this has been filled up for military reasons, so that exit from the Rājghāt Gate by wheeled vehicles is impossible. To the south of this road, and close to the city wall, are a number of small houses, one of which was, in 1857, the office of the Inland Transit Company, which managed the "dāk-ghārry" service; when the bridge of boats lay opposite the gate here, this situation was a convenient one for the office. The other houses along the wall were occupied by the Baptist minister, conductors, clerks, and pensioners, nearly all of whom, with their wives and families, were killed.

The Cantonment Gardens, on the right of the Rājghāt Gate road, were once covered by the "lines" of the Bengal Sappers and Miners; after their removal to Roorkee, about 1852, the huts were cleared away, and the camping-ground was here.

The road along the east of the gardens leads to a double-storied house, the residence, in 1857, of the Nawāb of Jhajjar. Close to this is a turning into the grounds of the Native Infantry Mess-house, once the residence of Shams-ud-din, Nawāb of Firozpur, and afterwards of one Ali Baksh Khān, who made a garden in the river-bed below. Between the mess-house and the road to the Khairāti Gate there is the mosque, called Zinat-ul-Masājid, the "Beauty among Mosques," built in 1710 by a daughter of Aurangzeb, who was buried in an adjoining tomb surrounded by a black-stone enclosure; she died in 1720.

Beyond the road to the Khairāti Gate is the Native Infantry Hospital, used for the same purpose in 1857, and guarded on the day of the outbreak by the Rifle Company of the 38th Light Infantry. Next to this is a house, No. 5, the entrance to which is rather hidden; in the garden-wall of the house are built two "bells-of-arms," belonging, in 1857, to the king's personal troops: the road then ran nearer to the house. This house bears evidence of being an old "bārahdari," having twelve doors to the centre room, around which other rooms were built afterwards. It had been the residence of the Rāja of Kishangarh, and it was here that Mr. Fraser dined with the rāja on the night of his murder.

In 1857 the house was occupied by a Mr. Aldwell, a Government pensioner; his son, who is still alive, can tell the story of a stubborn defence by a small body of people in the face of a considerable body of rebel Sepoys, aided by the rabble of Delhi and several guns. After two nights of attack the odds became too great, and there was not a drop of water to be had, so the little garrison decided to escape. Only Mr. Aldwell and his son were able to do so, the remainder being taken prisoners, and shot on the edge of a ditch, which runs through the infantry lines; into this their bodies were thrown. Mrs. Aldwell and her daughters had previously been smuggled out, and were taken into the palace, where they again escaped death when the other poor people were massacred in the court of the Nakkār Khāna.

Nearly opposite this house, on a rising ground, is a house, then the residence of the Rāja of Ballabgarh. There is nothing of importance in the Fāiz Bāzār, on the other side of the "lines," except the canal, which is said to have been made in the days of Firoze Shāh: how the water was brought to it is uncertain.

JĀMA MASJID.—This great mosque was commenced about 1650, and occupied five thousand workmen for the space of six years. The courtyard measures as much as four hundred feet each way, and the minarets are a hundred and thirty feet high; altogether, the building is of noble dimensions. The northern minaret was struck by lightning, but was repaired about 1817. The eastern gateway is considered still to be the Royal Gate, and is only opened for the highest personages; but on the steps collect the buyers and sellers of doves, for the people of Delhi are very fond of pets, and especially of fat-tailed sheep.

The ceremonies performed during prayer may here be described.

First, it is necessary to perform most careful ablutions, and then the worshippers form up in rows, facing towards Mecca, which is represented by an arched niche in the western hall, called the "mihrāb." Prayers are commenced while standing with the hands at the side; then the hands are raised on either side of the head, the thumbs touching the ear-lobes; then they are lowered and clasped in front of the body.

Now the body is bent, the hands resting on the knees; then the body is raised erect again. Next, the worshipper kneels and prostrates himself, the nose and forehead being made to touch the ground in that order; this is done two or three times, the worshipper sitting on the heels between each prostration. Lastly, he sits on the left foot, and, holding his hands in front as if they held a book, he recites a chapter of the Korān, finishing by turning the head right and left, and making a short supplication. While in each position a short prayer is said. On Fridays, formerly, the "khatbah" was read, which was a prayer for the reigning emperor, and recounted his titles, possibly including also his predecessors; but now the sermon follows, the imām preaching from the middle step of the pulpit. On occasion, the reigning British Emperor of India is prayed for.

The "āzān," or call to prayer, is made by several muezzins, who stand in the colonnades around the court, facing towards Mecca, their hands raised on either side of the head, the fore-fingers in the ears, to shut out worldly sounds, and also to increase the power of the voice. The call is as follows, each sentence being repeated :—

"God is great. I bear witness that Allāh is God. Mahomed is the Prophet of God. Haste to prayer, haste to salvation. (In the morning only, here is added, 'Prayer is better than sleep.') God is great. Allāh is the only God."

The weird cadence of their cries has a peculiar spell even over the believer in another religion; the Mahomedan may be said to be the most earnest in prayer among professors of any religion of the world.

CORONATION DARBĀR PARK.—About a quarter of a mile to the north of the Najafgarh Jhil Drain, a road to the right leads out of the Alipur Road to the site of the Proclamation of Edward the Seventh, the first British Emperor of India. There still remains the amphitheatre of earth, which was then covered with seats, and roofed in imitation of the Moghal style. An embankment has been thrown up all around to keep out the water, which floods the low-lying site during the rainy season, and the whole of the interior has been laid out as a park. An obelisk is to be erected in the centre to record the important event, which took place here on the first day of 1903.

BATTLEFIELD OF BADLI-KI-SARĀI.—About a mile beyond the village of Azādpur, where the Alipur Road joins the old Grand Trunk Road, is an old caravan-sarāi, built for the benefit of travellers by some old king. The road used to pass through this sarāi, but when converted into the Grand Trunk Road it was taken outside to the east. Just to the north of the village are two mounds, and an old building, which looks like a tomb. On the nearer mound is a grave, that of an officer killed during the battle. On this mound the enemy had posted their heavy guns, which opened with deadly effect on our troops advancing up the road, at the first flush of dawn, on June 8, 1857. On the west of the battlefield the railway runs, and beyond may be discerned trees which mark the Shāhlimār Gardens, laid out by Shāh Jahān in 1653; here was the first halting-place of the emperor in his progress to the Punjāb or to Cashmere. Beyond the gardens runs the canal, along the further bank of which the cavalry and guns made their turning movement, delayed by flooded country and numerous watercourses. Standing on the mound we can imagine the desperate charge of the 75th Foot, straight at the guns, although formed in square, the wild British cheer, the bayonetting of the gunners, and the pursuit to the walls of the sarāi, within which many a Sepoy fell.

GARDEN OF MAHALDĀR KHĀN.—The Grand Trunk Road, on the way to Delhi from Badli-ki-Sarāi, passes through a triple gateway, and just avoids another gate a few hundred yards distant. Between these two gates there used to be a bāzār, and the gates were built by one Mahaldār Khān, in the reign of Mahomed Shāh, about A.D. 1728. The garden of this noble is close by, and is one of the numerous ones which line the road, on either side, right up to the Sabzimandi.

ROSHANĀRA GARDEN.—A cross-road, from near a flour-mill, built on the site of the Sabzimandi Piquet, leads to the pleasant gardens laid out by the Sirhindi Begam, wife of Shāh Jahān, and by Roshanāra Begam, favourite sister of Aurangzeb. The latter is buried in the summer-house; she died in 1663.

MITHĀI BRIDGE.—The origin of this name, which is given to the bridge over the canal nearest to the Cābul Gate, is uncertain, but we find it mentioned in the account of the massacre of Nādir Shāh, long before the British occupation.

A road runs from here along the junction canal towards Old Delhi, and passes the end of the populous suburb known as the Sadr Bāzār; the suburb near the bridge is called the "Teliwāra Mandi," or Oil-sellers Market.

Hindu Rāo's House.—This was built as a residence by a Mr. William Fraser, agent to the governor-general at Delhi, about 1830. It stands in a splendid position, overlooking the city, and is open to any breeze which may blow. His murder has frequently been mentioned, and the story may now be told.

Mr. Fraser incurred the enmity of Shams-ud-din, then Nawāb of Firozpur, a small place which lies near the border of the Punjāb and the United Provinces. There are two accounts of how this bad feeling arose. The English account is that the nawāb was a dissolute young ruffian, and objected strongly to the admonitions of Fraser; the native account says that Mr. Fraser had formed too close a friendship with a young woman, who was the nawāb's relative, or his particular fancy: this story is embodied in a song of the dancing-girls of Delhi to this day. Whatever the real cause may have been, the young nawāb determined to rid himself of Mr. Fraser, and to this end suborned some assassins, who took up their residence in the "Billimori" (the "Bulvemar's Ward" of Colonel Sleeman); this street leads out of the Chāndni Chouk. For a long time the assassins sought their opportunity, but could find none. At last Mr. Fraser accepted an invitation to dine with the Rāja of Kishengarh, in Dariāganj, and returned to his house after dark. He took the road through the Mori Gate, and then followed the eastern side of the Ridge, turning up the winding road just below his house. At the turn in the road one of the murderers, who had been riding in front, turned his horse and shot Mr. Fraser as he passed him; he then galloped past the escort into the city, but was eventually caught and hanged. It is said, however, that the real murderer was concealed among the bushes, and from there fired the fatal shot; that he escaped into the Alwar State, and never met his deserts. The nawāb was tried for complicity, and was hanged outside the Cashmere Gate on October 10, 1835; his hanging body turned to the west, whereupon the people considered him to have been a martyr.

The house was then bought from the executors of Mr. Fraser by Hindu Rāo, a Mahratta nobleman, brother of the Bāiza Bāi, widow of Mahārāja Daulat Rāo Scindia of Gwalior. She had ascended the throne at her husband's death, but after nine years was deposed, and with her brother fled to the protection of " John Company." Hindu Rāo had resided for some years in Kishanganj before he bought this house, and here he transferred his hunting cheetas, which were one of the sights. It is a curious fact that the heavy fire directed on this house from Kishanganj, in 1857, came from his former residence. Hindu Rāo had died before that time. but the house was still occupied, when the Mutiny broke out, by his relatives. It has since been repaired, and is the property of Government, being used in the unhealthy season, which follows the rains, as a sanatorium for British soldiers from the fort.

At the back of the house is an old "baoli," supposed to date from pre-Mahomedan times, but the other old buildings around are part of Firoze Shāh's hunting-palace. Near the "Observatory" is a bench-mark of the Great Trigonometrical Survey; the name has probably been given to the building owing to this circumstance.

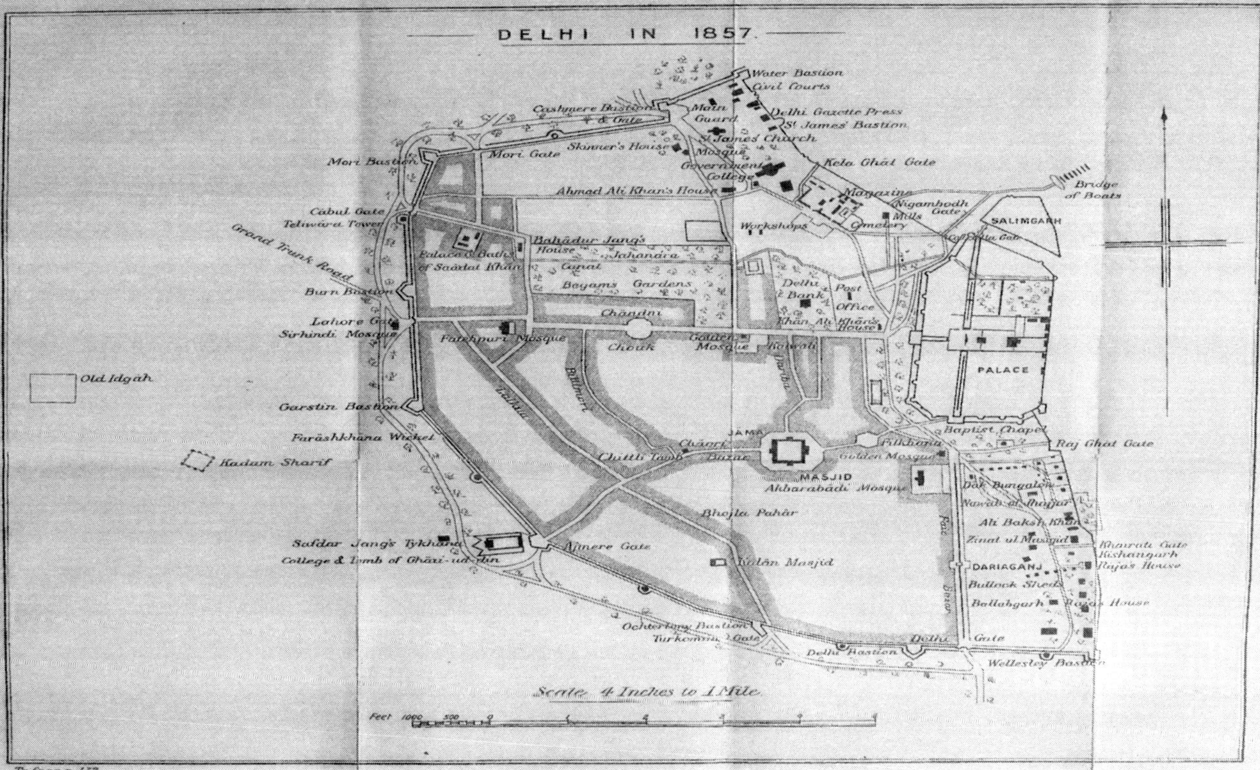
DELHI IN 1857
Water Bastion
Civil Courts
Cashmere Bastion
& Gate
Main Guard
Delhi Gazette Press
St James' Bastion
St James' Church
Skinner's House
Mosque
Government College
Kela Ghât Gate
Mori Bastion
Mori Gate
Ahmad Ali Khan's House
Magazine
Nigambodh Gate
Mills
Bridge of Boats
SALIMGARH
Cabul Gate
Teliwâra Tower
Workshops
Cemetery
Grand Trunk Road
Bahâdur Jang's House
Jahanâra
Palace & Baths of Saâdat Khan
Canal
Begams Gardens
Burn Bastion
Delhi Bank
Post Office
Chândni
Khan Ali Khân's House
Lahore Gate
Sirhindi Mosque
Fatehpuri Mosque
Chouk
Golden Mosque
Kotwali
PALACE
Old Idgâh
Garstin Bastion
Farâshkhâna Wicket
JAMA
MASJID
Baptist Chapel
Raj Ghât Gate
Kadam Sharif
Chitli Qabr
Chânri Bazar
Filkhana
Golden Mosque
Akbarabâdi Mosque
Dâk Bungalow
Bhojla Pahâr
Ali Baksh Khân
Zinat ul Masjid
Khairati Gate
Kishangarh Raja's House
Safdar Jang's Tykhâna
College & Tomb of Ghâzi-ud-din
Ajmere Gate
Kalân Masjid
DARIAGANJ
Bullock Sheds
Bullabgarh
Raja's House
Ochterlony Bastion
Turkoman Gate
Delhi Gate
Delhi Bastion
Wellesley Bastion
Fair Bazar
Scale 4 Inches to 1 Mile
Feet 1000 500 0 1 2 3 4

To face p. 172.

CHAPTER VIII

DELHI BEFORE THE MOGHAL CONQUEST

Mahomedan conquest of Delhi—The first Mahomedan king of India—The slaves who became kings—Altamsh—Balban—The Khilji dynasty—Alā-ud-din—Tughlak Shāh—His son Mahomed—Firoze Shāh—Timur's invasion—The Lodi kings—The Moghals called in.

IT is unnecessary to recapitulate the scanty history of Delhi before the Mahomedan conquest of the place, for that has been dealt with in the third chapter. The Mahomedan conqueror of India was Muiz-ud-din, Mahomed bin Sām, Shāhab-ud-din, commonly known as Mahomed of Ghor, the country from which he came. His first attempt ended in utter failure, for Prithwi Rāja, of Delhi, decisively defeated him at Tilauri, near Thanesar, in A.D. 1191. But he was not to be baulked in his design, came again after a year, and was completely successful, defeating and slaying on the same field the Hindu king. Kutb-ud-din Ibak, his general, proceeded to Delhi and occupied the place, entering the city on the west by the Ranjit Gate, the name of which was altered to the Ghazni Gate. Kutb-ud-din was appointed Indian Viceroy, but Mahomed of Ghor was sovereign, until he was murdered, in A.D. 1206, by a band of the Ghakkar tribe on the banks of the Indus.

On the death of Mahomed his kingdom was split up, and KUTB-UD-DIN became independent sovereign of India; he had been a slave, but had raised himself to be general, viceroy, and then first King of India. The dynasty which commenced with him is known as the "Slave Dynasty," for many of his successors, like himself, raised themselves from a condition of servitude to the throne. During his viceroyalty he had commenced the erection of the Kutb Minār, and had started, in 1200, the mosque which is close by; the former had not been completed when he met his death by a fall from his horse in A.D. 1210, while playing polo at Lahore, to which place he had removed his court. Possibly he was buried there, for his grave is not traceable at Delhi, unless it be one of some nameless ones in the courtyard of his mosque. He is said to have built himself a "White Palace" within the citadel, but no trace of this remains, although it is mentioned more than once in subsequent history.

Kutb-ud-din was succeeded by his son, ĀRĀM

SHĀH, a weak person, not at all fit to assume the reins, which indeed he soon had to resign to a stronger hand.

SHAMS-UD-DIN ALTAMSH, OR ILTITMISH, was a very different man, and the greatest of his dynasty. His story reminds us, to some extent, of Joseph, for his brethren sold him into slavery, and he was carried to Bokhāra. From there he was eventually brought to Delhi, and Kutb-ud-din gave for him the huge price of fifty thousand pieces of silver. His beauty is said to have been extraordinary, his valour and wisdom no less, and a valiant action on his part obtained for him his freedom, the post of captain-general, the hand of his master's daughter, and favour in the highest degree. At the time of his master's death he was Governor of Budāon, and when the inefficiency of Ārām Shāh became apparent he advanced on Delhi, possessed himself of the capital almost without a struggle, and ascended the throne in A.D. 1211.

The most important event of his reign was the arrival at Delhi in 1229 of an emissary from the Cāliph of Bāghdād, descendant of the Prophet, bearing a diploma which recognized Altamsh as an independent sovereign. Another event was a Moghal invasion, under Changiz Khān, the first attempt of this Central Asian tribe to obtain a footing; this they were unable to accomplish permanently until over three centuries had elapsed. To Altamsh we owe the completion of the Kutb Minār and an extension of the mosque enclosure, while his tomb, whether it was his own work or not, is certainly one of the most beautifully ornamented buildings of any age. He died in A.D. 1235.

Altamsh had no faith in the power of his sons to rule wisely, and said openly that he wished his daughter, Riziyat, to succeed him. This, however, she was not allowed to do immediately, for RUKN-UD-DIN FIROZE SHĀH first ascended the throne, the queen-mother being practically regent. This state of affairs did not long continue, for the daughter deposed him, amid the acclamation of the populace. He was imprisoned, and died in 1237, and was buried at Mālikpur, to the west of Old Delhi.

RIZIYAT was the only Queen of India until our own Queen Victoria assumed the title of Empress. She ruled, for a time, most wisely, and although she had ascended the throne without the countenance of the prime minister, or of the governors of the outlying districts, she was able to become mistress of her kingdom, and to earn for herself the manly title of "Sultān." Unfortunately, she was not equally wise where her heart was concerned, and disgusted her generals by showing favour to an Abyssinian slave, whom she made master of her horse, and also master of her heart. Probably she could not have pleased every one in her choice of a consort, but this action put all against her, and rebellion was not long in breaking out. In A.D. 1239 the governor of Sirhind took the field against her; she was defeated, and her Abyssinian lover was killed in the battle which ensued. The victor took her as wife, but the other generals would not brook this. They combined together, with the result that she and her new husband were defeated, and had to fly, but were overtaken and put to death in A.D. 1240. Her grave is now pointed out near the Turkmān Gate of the modern city, and the river once flowed close by.

Her brother, MUIZ-UD-DIN BAHRĀM SHĀH, succeeded, but he was miserably weak, as his father had foreseen, and the nobles revolted against him also, eventually murdering him in A.D. 1242; he was buried near his brothers at Mālikpur.

A son-in-law of the old king ascended the throne, but was deposed, in the evening of his coronation day, by ALĀ-UD-DIN MUSAUD SHĀH, son of Rukn-ud-din, and grandson of Altamsh.

His reign was a little longer than that of Bahrām Shāh, but was a troubled one, marked by two Moghal invasions; on the approach of the defending armies they retired. The king, considering himself safe, began to indulge in debauchery, injustice, and oppression, until the usual revolt deposed him in 1246, and he ended his days in prison. His tomb is unknown.

The family of Altamsh was not yet exhausted, and a third son, Nasr-ud-din Māhmud Ghori, came to the throne. He seems to have been a kindly man, better fitted for a hermitage than for a palace; but he had an excellent minister, Balban, who was also a very efficient general, and faithfully served his master—an uncommon thing in those days. The sultān esteemed his minister so highly that he actually married his daughter. Thanks to Balban, the kingdom of Delhi was now in a most flourishing condition, frequent expeditions meeting with entire success, and the borders being extended; the invading Moghals were repulsed, and lesser princes found a refuge from them in Delhi. The grandson of Changiz Khān, after taking Bāghdād and overthrowing the khālifate, sent an embassy to Māhmud. On this occasion an army was drawn up for review, consisting of nearly three hundred thousand horse and foot, with many war-elephants.

As the envoy moved towards the palace he found, at the city gate, some stuffed skins of Hindus—a hint of what might be the fate of captive Moghals. The scene in the king's darbār was a brilliant one, many Hindu rājas and refugee princes, in magnificent attire, standing round the throne. The walls of Delhi saw a hostile army, under a revolted vassal, in 1257; but the wise minister was on the alert against treason within, the gates were closed, and the traitors fled when the royal army sallied out.

Māhmud was a simple liver, made his queen cook for him, and kept no female slaves, but he did not disdain to build himself a new palace; this was on the banks of the Jumna, near Kilokri, but was probably a small one; his successors added to it. He died in A.D. 1266, after a reign of twenty years, leaving no male issue; and what more natural than that the minister, who had preserved the kingdom, should now mount the throne in the White Palace at Old Delhi? Ibn Batuta, writing seventy years after, declares that he murdered his master; but this, we hope, is a mistake.

GHIĀS-UD-DIN BALBAN, or Ulagh Khān, had been a slave, for he was made prisoner by the Moghals, whom he therefore had good reason to dislike; after various vicissitudes an agent of Altamsh bought him in a lot of a hundred slaves, and carried him to Delhi. According to Ibn Batuta, Balban was a miserable-looking creature, and Altamsh refused to take him. Balban then plucked up courage to ask him, "Why have you bought all these slaves?" Altamsh replied with a smile, "For my own sake, without doubt." Whereupon Balban said, "Then buy me for the sake of God," and Altamsh good-naturedly agreed to do so. He was not considered good-looking enough to be anything but a cup-bearer, but he joined a confederacy of forty slaves; by their efforts and his talents he raised himself to the highest place in the kingdom. Unfortunately, he now had to put out of the way all the survivors of this confederacy, but after this he reigned with justice and mercy. He bears a great name for generosity, and assigned princely allowances to fifteen petty sovereigns who sought his protection against the Moghals; he kept up great pomp and magnificence at his court, but was himself free from the vices so common among the monarchs of those days. A great sportsman, he kept his army engaged, and in good fighting trim, by making them beat for him while he was out hunting; his enemies thoroughly understood why he did so. Yet he could not prevent internal rebellion nor Moghal invasion; but all attempts came to naught in face of his good generalship, and that of his sons. Amongst other rebellions, which he quelled with a ruthless hand, was one among the Mewātis, a Rājput tribe, occupying the country to the south of Delhi. Nightly they plundered the suburbs, and were a source of great annoyance, but they were almost exterminated, and the remainder were forcibly converted to Islām; Mahomedan they remain to this day.

While he was still minister, he built a red palace, which is said to have been in Old Delhi. Another account places it near the tomb of Nizām-ud-din Auliā, within the fort of Marzgan, which was built by Balban, and was sometimes called Ghiāspur. He died in A.D. 1287, and his tomb, a complete ruin, is near the Jamāli Masjid.

Balban had selected for the succession one of his grandsons, Kāi Khusru; but an intrigue placed another grandson, Muiz-ud-din Kāi Kubād, on the throne. The principal noble had conceived a strong enmity to Kāi Khusru, and had recourse to stratagem to supplant him. He forged a letter, purporting to be the decision of the other nobles, and stating that they had elected Kāi Kubād king; with this he repaired to Kāi Khusru by night, and advised him to escape. To this counsel Kāi Khusru was foolish enough to listen; he was passed out of the city by the treacherous noble, who forthwith went to Kāi Kubād, acquainted him of the stratagem, and proclaimed him emperor.

This prince had many good parts, had a considerable taste for literature, and had been very strictly brought up, but now he gave himself up to the full enjoyment of pleasure, would not attend to the affairs of the kingdom, and retired to the palace at Kilokri (near Humāyun's tomb) to enjoy himself thoroughly in the company of those who could best minister to his pleasures. He did not desire to be bothered with state matters; any one who would relieve him of his power was welcome to it. The Moghals thought this a favourable hour for a fresh invasion, but they were defeated, and then the foolish king was persuaded to order a general massacre of the Moghal mercenaries in his employ. The employment of Moghals in Indian armies was quite a usual practice.

Kāi Kubād's father had all this while been Viceroy of Bengal, content to be the vassal of his own son. He now endeavoured to awake him to a sense of his duty, and succeeded, but Kāi Kubād's repentance was short-lived, and fresh pleasures alone filled his mind. Such a state of affairs could have but one end, in the shape of revolt. Shāista Khan, Governor of Samāna and prime minister, advanced on Delhi, and at this moment the king succumbed to his bad habits, and became paralyzed. An infant son was placed on the throne, but the sons of Shāistā Khān boldly cut their way through the royal army, and carried off the young prince. The avenging force, issuing through the Budāon Gate, was restrained from pursuit by fear of his assassination by his captors. Meanwhile an assassin had been sent to Kilokri, and Kāi Kubād had been murdered; his body was thrown out of the palace window on to the sands of the river below. Shāistā Khān ascended the throne, and the infant prince was put to death soon afterwards; this happened in A.D. 1290.

Shāistā Khān was one of the Khiljis, a tribe occupying part of Central Asia, in the vicinity of Ghor, and the dynasty which now follows is known by this name. He was seventy years of age when he mounted the throne in the White Palace, and assumed the name of JALĀL-UD-DIN. After the murder of the young prince, and the removal of a possible rival, he ruled with great lenity, his only other reprehensible act being the murder of a mulla. The mulla appealed to him for mercy, but he hesitated to pardon him; as a rule, however, he hesitated to punish. The death of the mulla was followed by a fearful famine in Delhi.

When the king was in Delhi he occupied the Red Palace of Balban, but he did not care to reside within the walls, apparently distrusting the inhabitants, who, however, soon became reconciled to his rule. He usually resided at Kilokri, building there a Green Palace, in addition to enlarging and beautifying the existing palace of his predecessor. His nobles also built houses in the vicinity, but all have crumbled into dust.

The lenity of Jalāl-ud-din was little appreciated, for robbers increased in number, and the Moghals again invaded in great strength; the king was uniformly successful against them, but did not follow up his successes or adequately punish the evil-doers. His nephew, Alā-ud-din, was ruthless enough, and added large territories to the kingdom, on which he now set his heart. The king was old, but the slow approach of a natural death was not what Alā-ud-din desired, so intrigues were set on foot, the king was induced to visit the camp at Karra, and, as he grasped the hand of his nephew, he was murdered, in a boat on the Ganges, in the year 1296. His tomb at Delhi is mentioned by Firoze Shāh, but no trace remains.

ALĀ-UD-DIN, also called Sikandar Sāni (the second Alexander), though crowned at Karra, was not to ascend the throne at Delhi without at least a show of force, for the widow of Jalāl-ud-din placed her son on the throne in the Green Palace at Kilokri. But when the army of Alā-ud-din encamped outside the north-east gate of Old Delhi, after a march in the rainy season, there was only a parade in battle array, and the opposing army was withdrawn within the walls. Desertions naturally followed, and Alā-ud-din was able to enter in triumph; he proceeded to the Red Palace of Balban, where he ascended the throne. To please his subjects he distributed largess from catapults, and organized games, thus becoming the object of admiration, instead of detestation on account of his crime. His rival cousin had fled to Multān, but was there invested; he was captured, brought to Delhi with his brother, blinded, and soon afterwards murdered in prison at Hānsi.

Once again the Moghals invaded the Punjāb, once again they were defeated with great loss, and a massacre of prisoners followed at Delhi, women and children not being spared. On returning from an expedition into Guzerāt the mercenary Moghal soldiery revolted, but they were defeated, and the king, who had remained at Delhi, ordered a wholesale massacre of their families, who occupied a suburb called Moghalpur; very different was he from his lenient old uncle.

These proceedings awakened the resentment of the Moghals beyond the frontier, who, after sustaining one defeat, advanced in a great horde to the vicinity of Delhi. This was a business for the king to deal with, for no one else would undertake the task, although the streets were filled with refugees, and panic and famine raged. He therefore marched out of the Budāon Gate with a vast army, drew it up on the plains beyond the suburbs which stretched to the north-east, and joined battle with complete success, although the pursuit was not carried out with vigour, owing to jealousy among his generals.

Alā-ud-din now proceeded to extend his dominions. He had hardly set out, when he was severely wounded in a treacherous attempt at assassination; fortunately he had the strength to appear before his army, who acclaimed him, and the would-be supplanter had to flee. But more rebellion followed, and on one occasion the rebels managed to seize a great portion of Delhi; all attempts, however, ended in failure, and no pardon was ever extended to any of those who took part, even their families being put to death. At last, in A.D. 1300, the king began to think that he himself might be to blame for the frequent conspiracies against him, and, on the advice of a council of nobles, relaxed his severities. He contemplated the formation of a new religion, and therefore saw that his nobles reformed their ways, not to his disadvantage, for he confiscated their ill-gotten gains.

While he was away from Delhi, on an expedition into Bengal, the Moghals saw their chance, and raided right up to the walls. Alā-ud-din hastened back, but had to leave his cavalry behind. He could do nothing but entrench his army round Shāhpur, and send urgent messages to the provincial governors for reinforcements. The Moghals were, however, in a position to intercept these, and matters looked very black until, after two months of inaction, the Moghals suddenly retired, some say in a panic brought about by the miraculous powers of Nizām-ud-din, the saint. This was in A.D. 1303. Upon the retirement of the invaders Alā-ud-din commenced the building of the city of Siri, the erection within it of a "palace of a thousand pillars," and the repair or reconstruction of the walls of the citadel of Old Delhi. He also prepared to punish the Moghals, and began to collect a vast army for the purpose. He is said to have been able to put

475,000 horse into the field, but the expense of keeping them overtaxed the prosperity of his kingdom.

Nothing daunted, the Moghals again advanced, but Tughlak, one of Alā-ud-din's generals, of whom we shall hear more, defeated them with great slaughter. Many chiefs were taken prisoner and sent to Delhi to be trodden to death by elephants. Again and again, in 1305 and 1306, the Moghal hordes crossed swords with Tughlak, but only to send more captives to be slaughtered at Delhi; their heads were piled in heaps or built into the foundations of new buildings. When their continued ill-success caused them to desist, the war was carried into their own country, and the fame of Tughlak grew with each of his twenty-nine victories.

Another general of Alā-ud-din, Mālik Kafur, was very successful in the south; he had been a slave, for whom the king had paid a thousand dinārs. Later, he returned from Bengal with rich spoils, which he laid at the feet of his master as he sat at the Budāon Gate. An expedition into the Deccan was even more successful, the royal booty being enormous, while the private soldiers threw away silver, as being too cumbersome; it is said that the king distributed a portion of the spoils, so that the sum-total must have been very great indeed. But his displeasure fell on the Moghal mercenaries, and he discharged them. Some, who were in great need, and almost starving, conspired against him, with the result that a wholesale massacre was ordered, in which fifteen thousand perished, and none were spared.

Alā-ud-din was now at the zenith of his power, and devoted himself to the building of monuments, amongst others the unfinished minār, which was to have been double the height of the other, and yet perhaps not sufficiently high to represent his overweening pride. But now he fell sick, Mālik Kafur began to intrigue against him, rebellion broke out in the Deccan and in Guzerāt. The king, unable to repress it himself, and seeing his general defeated, died of his disorder, aggravated by rage and grief, in A.D. 1316. He was buried in his palace, now in ruins, at the south-west of the Kuwwat-ul-Islām Mosque.

Amongst other buildings of his, not previously mentioned, is an unfinished mosque in Siri; the Hāuz Khās was also his work. Ferishta well says of him, " If we look upon the policy of Alā-ud-din, a great king arises to our view. If we behold his hands, which are red, an inexorable tyrant appears. He began in cruelty, and waded through blood to the end," enlisting in his designs, we may add, the very elephants, which he armed with dreadful weapons, so that they might torture the wretched victims of his wrath. But yet "his pomp, wealth, and power were never equalled by any prince who sat before him on the throne of Hindustān."

On the death of the king, Mālik Kafur raised to the throne the youngest son, SHĀHAB-UD-DIN OMAR, with a view to controlling the kingdom himself as regent; to this end he produced a spurious will of the deceased monarch. But his inhuman cruelties, directed against the other sons of Alā-ud-din, caused the commander of the guards to plot against him, and assassinate him thirty-five days after. Firoze Shāh was of opinion that he was a faithful servant, and restored his tomb, but history dwells rather on his cruelties. The puppet king was now deposed, and the third son of the late king, KUTB-UD-DIN MUBĀRIK SHĀH, was released from prison and the instant fear of being blinded. He gained over all the nobles and ascended the throne, depriving his brother of any chance of regaining the throne by blinding him, for a blind man was ever considered unfit to be sultān. Perhaps we may consider him to have been merciful in not depriving his brother of his life also.

The king now proceeded to thoroughly enjoy himself, and is actually reported to have dressed himself as a dancing-girl, and to have performed in the houses of the nobility. He then raised to power one Khusru Khān, a Hindu renegade, and would listen to no cautions against his favourite, with the almost inevitable result that Khusru plotted against his life and kingdom. The plot was only too successful, and the wretched king was murdered in a scuffle, in which Khusru took the principal part. He had completed the walls of Old Delhi, the repairs of which were commenced by his father, but no other work of his remains. His grave was repaired, amongst others of the sons of Alā-ud-din, by Firoze Shāh; it was probably within his father's mausoleum, for none of his successors can have erected one in his honour.

The murder of the king took place in A.D. 1320, and KHUSRU KHĀN seated himself on his throne, forcibly marrying his widow, Dewal Devi, a Hindu princess. He assumed the ridiculous title (for a ruffian, who was renegade only for his own ends, and despised his adopted creed) of Nasr-ud-din, or supporter of religion. But not for long was he allowed to occupy the throne, for he disgusted every one by using the Korān for a seat, he prohibited the slaughter of cattle, and reverted to his former religion. Tughlak, therefore, advanced on Delhi, with an army which had been trained by constant war against the Moghals. The force sent against him by Khusru was easily dispersed, and Tughlak appeared before the walls, the usurper drawing out his army, and entrenching it near the Hāuz Khās. In spite of liberal largess, his troops began to desert him, and an action, though partly successful, made it clear that his was a lost cause. Khusru therefore fled towards Tilpat, his adherents dropping away as he went, and he was found on the following day concealed in a tomb, whence he was dragged to his death, which none regretted. The keys of the capital were delivered to the victor, and, when he inquired if there was any prince of the previous dynasty alive, he was hailed as king. Thus commenced another dynasty, in A.D. 1320.

GHIAS-UD-DIN TUGHLAK SHĀH had commenced life as a slave, and had been brought from Khorāssān to Delhi in the time of Alā-ud-din. As we have seen, he was appointed "Warden of the Marches," and had showed excellent generalship; he was also Governor of Dipālpur and Lahore. He soon afterwards commenced the new city of Tughlukābād. While engaged in building it an army sent by him to the Deccan was dispersed by a rumour that he had died, some declaring that they had seen him buried; the men

TOMB OF TUGHLAK SHĀH.

[To face p. 19.

who started the rumour were caught and sent to Delhi, where the sarcastic old king ordered them to be buried alive. In A.D. 1323 he took the field, and made an expedition into Bengal; while he was away, his son Junā, left viceroy at Delhi, plotted against him, aided by the saint, Nizām-ud-din Auliā. As Tughlak approached Delhi, Junā invited him to rest in a pavilion erected at Afghānpur, and constructed in such a manner as to fall down if an elephant pressed against one of the pillars. Junā induced the favourite son to sit beside his father, and the elephants approached, with the result that the pavilion fell on those seated within, and crushed them to death.

Ibn Batuta says that the elephants were made to go up the steps to salute the king, so perhaps the whole structure toppled over; some, however, attributed the disaster to lightning, for to definitely accuse Junā with the deed might have met with awkward consequences. The manner of compassing this murder reminds us of the way in which the death of Agrippina was attempted by Nero, it being arranged that the heavy canopy of a boat should fall on her.

Tughlak Shāh died in 1325, and was buried outside his new city, in the outwork which he had constructed in the lake close by. His tomb is said by some to have been erected by his son Junā.

Junā Khān proceeded from Tughlukābād to Old Delhi, in order there to ascend the throne after the usual custom, assuming the title of MAHOMED IBN TUGHLAK; he is generally known as the "Khuni Sultān," or "Bloody King," for his cruelty was terrible. In many ways he resembled Nero, for, in spite of being a parricide, he seems to have had high aspirations and accomplishments, but relapsed into an insatiable lust for blood. He was a great patron of literature, a founder of colleges, a great builder, a good general; but while the suburbs of Delhi owed him protecting walls, he more than counterbalanced this by forcing the inhabitants to leave, as will be related. He seems almost at once to have abandoned his father's city, although he built a fort close by, which contained a "palace of a thousand pillars," and was called "Adilābād."

In the first year of his reign the cities of Delhi saw an invading horde of Moghals at their gates, and the suburbs were plundered freely. Mahomed had not the army to drive them off, but he somehow had money, and a heavy ransom induced the enemy to retire; Nizām-ud-din had probably died just previously. In 1328 he surrounded the suburbs between Siri and Old Delhi with walls, calling the city thus formed Jahān panāh, or the "shelter of the world." He now got together an army, and overran many countries, even contemplating an invasion of China; but his troops perished, almost to a man.

During an expedition to the Deccan Mahomed was much struck with the advantages of Deogiri, and determined to found a new capital there; he therefore, in 1338, ordered the inhabitants of Delhi to move there in a body, and, in order to make the journey more pleasant, he had trees planted all along the road. A revolt at Multān soon brought him back, and the people were also allowed to return; but in 1340 they had again to set out for Deogiri, and he saw that they had no inducement to remain by burning their houses. His troops, searching by his orders, found only a blind man and a cripple left; the latter was flung from a catapult, the former dragged along until his legs dropped off. In 1342 a dreadful famine raged in the Deccan, and the people were again permitted to return; but the famine was just as bad in Delhi, and men even ate each other, the famine continuing for two years, until the people petitioned to be allowed to migrate. In 1345 Delhi was again populated, and the inhabitants were allowed to remain undisturbed.

In 1343 an emissary had come from Egypt, as the result of a long negotiation, and brought with him a diploma from the descendant of the Abbaside khālifas. Mahomed conceived himself only now to be a rightful king, and ordered that those of his predecessors who had not received such sanction should not be mentioned in the "khatbah." Thus the names of all, as far back as Altamsh, were struck out, including even his own father. Egypt, it may be mentioned, passed under Turkish rule at the end of the sixteenth century, and it is to the Sultan of Turkey that Mahomedans now look as their spiritual head.

All this time, east, south, west, and north, rebellion was rife, but was invariably put down with a strong hand, and punished with barbarous severity. At length Mahomed had to undertake an expedition into Sind, and there he died, on the Indus, near Tatta, in A.D. 1351. Ferishta sums up his reign with the remark that "he seems to have laboured, with no contemptible abilities, to be detested by God, and feared and abhorred by all men."

Mahomed Tughlak left no son, so his generals elected to the throne FIROZE SHĀH TUGHLAK, a nephew of the founder of the dynasty, and son of a Hindu princess. He had been educated and brought up by his uncle, and had enjoyed the special favour of his cousin—favour for which he was not ungrateful. He caused the relatives of those whom his cousin had visited with cruelty, mutilation, or death, to be sought out, gave them compensation, obtained their acquittances, and placed the deeds in the grave, so that Mahomed, when he rises at the last day to proceed to judgment, might be able to show the acquittances to his Maker; in the grave the deeds may be resting to this day.

Firoze Shāh had at once to meet invading Moghals, whom he defeated; he then proceeded to Delhi, where he was met by the submissive inhabitants, whom he feasted and entertained on a large scale. He then had, as usual, to consolidate his kingdom, in the course of which work he twice moved into Bengal, and twice into Sind. On his return from his first Bengal expedition, he commenced, in 1354, his new city of Firozābād. Two years later, he ordered the cutting of the first canal of the many which now water the plains of India, and relieve the inhabitants of fear of famine. He may be called the "Father" of the Irrigation Department, for, alive to the advantages to his people of the water, he instituted a revenue system and appointed officials to collect it. His army he recruited from the sons and relatives of those of his soldiers who had to retire from age or infirmity, a system which largely obtains to-day. Although not a great king—indeed, rather a weak one—he was one of the most enlightened rulers that India has seen—kindly, courteous, and liberal, even if he had faults in religious bigotry, and an undue affection for wine. He endowed many colleges and hospitals, laid out many a garden and vineyard, and repaired the tombs and monuments of his predecessors in a manner which is emulated with some success to-day. He instituted the practice, copied afterwards by the Moghal emperors, of having three courts of audience—the outermost for the general public, the innermost for nobles and ministers of state, and the intermediate one for personal attendants and the better classes of the people. The Egyptian khālifa, unsolicited, sent him a robe of honour, and others for his son and for his minister.

He was also a great sportsman, and within his park, on the Ridge, he had a hunting-seat, a darbār hall (on the top of which there was a chiming clock), and a menagerie, with a small collection of "freaks." Many mosques were built during his reign, some by his minister Khān Jahān, a Hindu convert; the number includes the Chauburji Mosque, on the Ridge; the Kalān Masjid; the Jāma Masjid, in his kotila; the Sanjar and Jamāt Khāna Mosques, near the tomb of Nizām-ud-din Auliā; the Begampur Mosque, and the Khirki Mosque. The Kadam Sharif enclosure also dates from his reign, as does the shrine of Roshan Chirāgh Delhi. Altogether, it was a time of busy building, and the total population of Delhi must have been very great, for the old cities were not abandoned when Firozābād was occupied. He died in A.D. 1388, and was buried on the edge of the Hāuz Khās of Alā-ud-din.

There is a Hindi proverb to the effect that "human beings differ in their constitution; while the one is a diamond, the next is but a common stone." To say that Firoze Shāh was a diamond is, perhaps, to go too far; but his immediate successors were, by comparison, mere clods of earth. Firoze Shāh was succeeded by his grandson, GHIĀS-UD-DIN TUGHLAK SHĀH II., but he was shortly afterwards killed by the adherents of ABU BAKR SHĀH, his cousin. This king managed to establish himself in Firozābād, but his rule extended no further; the streets often saw fighting between his troops and those of Mahomed Shāh, his uncle, whom Firoze Shāh had at one time associated with himself as king.

At length intrigues resulted in the deposition of Abu Bakr and the proclamation of MAHOMED SHĀH as king, but he died shortly afterwards, and was buried with his father. The next king, SIKANDAR SHĀH, only reigned forty days, and then succumbed to a violent disorder in 1393.

The death of this king found no definite claimant to the throne, and the nobles decided on MĀHMUD, son of the late Mahomed Shāh. His power was visionary for a considerable time, and once he was actually shut out of, and had to lay siege to, his capital of Old Delhi. When he had reoccupied that city, intrigues lost him the city of Firozābād, where a rival king, NASR-UD-DIN NASRIT SHĀH, was set up. For about four years the plains between these two cities were witness of frequent engagements, which remind one of revolutions in South American republics to-day. First one, then the other got the advantage, and a perfectly astonishing state of affairs prevailed, which would take too long to describe. At length there came on the scene a common enemy, the great Moghal leader, Timur, so well known to us as Tamerlane.

The invading horde of Moghals crossed the Indus in A.D. 1398, and advanced without difficulty to Pānipat. A little below this town Timur crossed the Jumna (probably at Bāghpat), occupied the Fort of Loni, opposite Firozābād, and encamped on the bank of the river. He then, with a body of horse, crossed over and reconnoitred the palace on the Ridge. Having seen what he wanted, and repulsed an attack, he returned, and moved his camp to about opposite where Metcalfe House now stands. It was reported to him that the vast crowd of captives in his camp had watched with delight the attack which had been made on him. So he ordered that all should be put to the sword, lest they might be an embarrassment when the great battle should take place. With such enthusiasm did all take part in this bloody work, that a certain Moulvi killed, with his own hand, fifteen captives, although he had not previously lifted a weapon, even against a sheep. Timur's army then forded the river, and he entrenched his camp on the plains of Firozābād, digging a ditch and placing in front of it lines of buffaloes, tied together to break a charge. Two days afterwards, disregarding the protests of the astrologers, he marched out of this entrenchment and set his troops in battle array, about where Safdar Jang's tomb now stands. The Indian army moved to the attack courageously enough. There were twelve thousand horse, forty thousand foot, and the attack was led by a line of elephants, carrying on their backs towers filled with archers and slingers; in the intervals were crossbowmen. The veteran troops of Timur were considerably dismayed at the sight of the elephants, but firmly met the attack, repulsed it, and pursued the flying enemy to the gates of Old Delhi, which was abandoned during the night.

The next five days were spent by Timur in feasting by the side of the Hāuz Khās; but on the 17th of December—a Wednesday—he repaired to the idgāh which was in front of the Darwāza-i-Māidān Gate, towards the Hāuz Khās, and there received the submission of the principal inhabitants of the three cities, to whom he promised protection of life and property. The imperial standard was set up over the principal gate; two days after that, the Moulvi, whose hands were dyed with blood, pronounced from the pulpit of the cathedral mosque of Firozābād the names and titles of the conqueror.

But while this was going on the people were being put to the sword. Some of Timur's ladies had ridden into the city of Jahānpanāh to inspect the "Palace of a Thousand Pillars." The people feared an attack by the escort, and themselves brought on a scuffle, which resulted in a massacre for three whole days. The man who, in cold blood, could put harmless captives to death, was not likely to spare turbulent brawlers, even though innocent people might suffer with them. A band of Hindus took refuge in the mosque of Old Delhi, but found no sanctuary there, for on the fourth day they were slaughtered, and not one was spared. At length the massacre ceased; those who survived, and had not fled, were parted among the victors as slaves, and Timur reserved for himself all the stonemasons. He then entered the city and took possession of twelve rhinoceros, and the remainder of the menagerie, which had been collected by Firoze Shāh.

On the last day of 1398, Timur marched to Firozābād and inspected the mosque in the kotila of Firoze Shāh, with which he was delighted. He was here presented with two white parrots, supposed to be seventy-four years old, which had been transferred from one king to the next since the days of Tughlak Shāh. Timur then returned to Samarkand.

After two months of anarchy Nasrit Shāh crept back and took possession of the spoiled cities, almost destitute of inhabitants, who, however, soon began to return. He was shortly afterwards driven out by one of the nobles, Ikbāl Khān, who occupied Delhi, while the provinces were partitioned among other nobles. Māhmud then returned, at the invitation of Ikbāl, but foolishly deserted his only supporter, and did not resume the throne until he was summoned by Dāulat Khān Lodi, after Ikbāl Khān had been killed in action. In 1407 Māhmud was besieged in Firozābād by a revolted noble, Khizr Khān, but held out until the siege was raised for want of supplies. In 1411 he had again to shut himself up, this time in Siri, while Firozābād was occupied by the same enemy; but the siege was again raised. Māhmud died at last, in A.D. 1412, after a reign of over twenty years, without a shadow of power, and with an experience of ill-fortune such as has been the lot of few kings.

The nobles now elected DAULAT KHĀN LODI, but he was almost immediately besieged in the city of Siri by stronger forces than he had available. He had to surrender, after reigning a year, to KHIZR KHĀN, thus successful at the third attempt; with him commences the dynasty of the Sāyyads. For some reason or other, this king considered himself a vassal of Timur, and without solicitation sent tribute to Samarkand. He built, in 1418, a fort called Khizrābād, of which no trace remains; it may have been near Okhla. Otherwise his reign of seven years contains no event of interest. He died in 1421, and his mausoleum used to stand at Okhla, but was removed to make room for the Agra Canal.

TOMB OF MAHOMED SHĀH.

[To face p. 205

Mubārik Shāh, who succeeded, had a stormy reign, and was not often at Delhi, but towards the end of his reign, in 1433, he ordered the building of a new city on the bank of the river, to be called Mubarikābād. It was, however, never destined to be finished, for a plot was made against the king, and he was assassinated in the mosque which he had built within the lines of his city; his mausoleum also is there.

The last of the Sāyyad dynasty was Mahomed Shāh, son of Farid Khān, and grandson of Khizr Khān, the founder of the dynasty. His reign also was a troubled one, and sieges of the different cities of Delhi were common. In 1435 he was shut up in Siri, and was nearly murdered, only escaping by admitting the besiegers by the Bāghdād Gate. In 1440 the King of Mālwa invested Delhi, but was defeated by the valourous Bahlol Lodi, and retired. In 1441, however, Bahlol turned his powerful army against his master, and besieged him in Old Delhi for some months, but then had to abandon the enterprise. Mahomed died in 1445, and his tomb is one of the finest of the period; it has been noticed near the village of Khāirpur.

The son of Mahomed, Alam Shāh, can hardly be termed a king, for Delhi was almost his only possession, and that city he resigned for Badāon, where he abdicated in 1450, on condition that he should not be disturbed. So weak was he that he could not keep a yard of country south of Old Delhi, the village of Mahrāuli and the Lado Sarāi being in the hands of the Mewātis.

Another dynasty was now started by BAHLOL LODI, an Afghān, whose name we have noticed in the reigh of Mahomed Shāh; he it was, also, who drove out Alam Shāh. He consolidated his power by the imprisonment of the minister who had acquiesced in his coming to the throne, but spared his life, which was great generosity for those days. There were, however, other and equally strong claimants, and one, the King of Jāunpur, laid siege to Delhi in 1451, while Bahlol was absent. The siege was soon raised, mainly through intrigue, a principal noble being detached from the side of the besiegers, during an action, at a place thirty miles north of Delhi. Bahlol thus regained his capital, and none of the many expeditions made against the place by enemies got as far as the walls, although one army seems to have reached the Bhattiāra Fort, to the west. Towards the end of his reign Bahlol did not feel equal to continuing the constant struggle, and therefore divided up his kingdom among his enemies, retaining for his son only Delhi and some surrounding districts.

He died in A.D. 1488, and was buried in his own garden, opposite the enclosure of Roshan Chirāgh Delhi.

Nizām Khān, SIKANDAR LODI, succeeded his father, but not without a fight, for the Afghān nobles did not approve of the fact that he was son of a Hindu lady, the daughter of a goldsmith, and therefore not of noble blood. His rival was his cousin, but he managed to defeat him, and generously forgave him. Many expeditions followed, so that Sikandar was not able to return to Delhi until 1490, and there he could only halt for three weeks before he had to march again, in order to repress insurrection. He then spent years in other places, and in 1504 took a dislike to Delhi, because of the great sickness which had followed the heat of the previous year. He appointed a small commission to proceed down the Jumna and select a site for a new city; in their report they recommended Agra, and there he founded a capital, which, in the following year, was destroyed by a violent earthquake. He did not, however, abandon Agra, but rebuilt it, and it remained the capital of Sikandar and of his successors until the days of Shāh Jahān; no king, however, was considered properly crowned unless he ascended the throne at Delhi.

Sikandar died at Agra in 1518, but his body

was taken to Delhi and buried there, near Khāirpur. He seems to have spent very little of his long reign at Delhi, but he laid out a considerable sum in the repair of the ancient monuments, such as the Kutb Minār and the tomb of Firoze Shāh. At the commencement of his reign there was built the Moth-ki-Masjid, which is said to have been built out of funds provided by the sale of crops of pulse, originating from a single seed.

Sikandar was succeeded by his son, Ibrāhim Lodi, who ascended the throne at Agra. He was a man of a very haughty temperament, and made his nobles stand in front of him with their hands folded in a servile manner. This they would not brook, for the Afghāns considered that the king was only the principal noble, and entitled to the throne only so long as they chose. This fact accounts for the curious state of affairs, which existed from now onwards, until the Moghals had firmly established an empire, a thing they could not have done had not each Afghān noble considered his own interests only. Ibrāhim's reign was one long struggle against his nobles, until, in 1525, even his brother Alā-ud-din took the field against him, and invested Delhi with a large force. Ibrāhim, however, aided by fortune, managed to relieve the city, so Alā-ud-din, retiring to the Punjāb, called in Bābar, the

Moghal chief. Previously to this a brazen bull, taken in an expedition to the south, had been set up opposite the Bāghdād Gate of Siri.

Here we may commence a new chapter, in the course of which we shall see Delhi rise to the zenith of its splendour, and fall again, through many vicissitudes, to a comparatively unimportant position, with an extent of dependent territory, which was not more than a mere estate, the rents from which supplemented the king's pension from the Honourable East India Company.

CHAPTER IX

DELHI IN MOGHAL TIMES

Bābar—Humāyun—Akbar—Jahāngır—Shāh Jahān—Aurangzeb —Puppet emperors—Mahomed Shāh—Nadır Shāh's invasion —Ahmad Khān Abdālı—Mahratta predominance—Shāh Ālam—Ghulām Kādır—A blind emperor.

We have seen that the Moghals had persistently invaded India, from the days of Altamsh onward, with very little success, having often to retreat hurriedly. Timur, it is true, inflicted a severe defeat on Māhmud Shāh, and occupied the capital; but even he did not remain, and left the country to fall into a state of anarchy. A new kingdom had been built up by the Lodi kings out of the ruins; but the jealousy of the brother of Ibrāhim Lodi caused him to call in Bābar to his aid—a short-sighted policy in any case, for as well might a jackal call in a tiger to help him kill a cow, and expect him not to have his feed. The Moghals did not have matters all their own way, for the Afghān nobles were not the men to resign a fair heritage without a struggle;

MOGHAL EMPERORS.

[To face p. 210.

but from now onwards, with a short interregnum, Bābar and his descendants were Kings of Delhi until the last of the House of Timur died a deported prisoner in Rangoon, and an English Empress was proclaimed.

Zahir-ud-din Mahomed Bābar was descended from Changiz Khān, and belonged to the Chāgitai branch of the Moghal tribe. He was at this time King of Cābul, and had already undertaken four expeditions into India, but had always been recalled by trouble in his own kingdom, and had not penetrated further than Lahore. He now gladly seized the opportunity of carrying out a cherished project, and crossed the Indus, for the fifth time, in 1526, with a comparatively small force, numbering scarcely twelve thousand men. He had, however, one auxiliary arm, as yet unknown in India, which was his artillery, superintended by a Turk. He advanced rapidly, against little opposition, until Ibrāhim advanced to Pānipat to stop him, with an enormous army. Bābar remarks that it might have been much larger had Ibrāhim not been so parsimonious, for the wealth left to him by his father, Sikandar, was very great. However this may be, the large army he had collected must have seemed to him sufficient to overwhelm Bābar's little force; but the result proved otherwise. Ibrāhim was not much of a general, and drew up his army in one long line, expecting that the shock of one charge would be quite sufficient; but the Moghals stoutly withstood the charge, and bodies held in reserve made counter-attacks, which threw the Indian army into confusion. Ibrāhim, whose personal courage was without reproach, died fighting in a last charge, and five thousand dead lay around the spot where his body was found. The losses of his army exceeded sixteen thousand.

Bābar quickly followed up his victory, and hurried forward his son Humāyun to Agra, the capital of Ibrāhim. He himself marched on Delhi, and entered that city on April 24, 1526, three days after the battle. He had previously sent forward a detachment to secure the treasure and prevent plunder. Of his visit to Delhi he gives an account in his most interesting Memoirs; he mentions the shrine of Nizām-ud-din Auliā, that of Kutb-ud-din, the Hāuz-i-Shamsi (which is close to the latter), and the Hāuz Khās. He also visited the palace of Alā-ud-din and "his minaret," the sepulchres and gardens of Bahlol and Sikandar. He then embarked on a boat, and dropped down the river to Agra, drinking "arrack," which presumably he tasted for the first time. He was, however, well acquainted with the delights of the cup, and his ideas were well stated in his own words, "Enjoy freely, O Bābar, for life is not twice to be enjoyed."

Bābar never returned to Delhi alive, but his remains were borne through on their journey to Cābul, after they had been interred for a time at Agra. Humāyun, his son, had previously returned to Cābul; on his way he had broken open the treasury at Delhi, and had helped himself, to the great indignation of his father, who wrote him a severe lecture.

Nasr-ud-din Mahomed Humāyun succeeded his father in A.D. 1530, but at once resigned, to his brother Kāmrān, the provinces beyond the Indus, the Punjāb, and Hissār-Firoza. Although he thus saved himself a certain amount of trouble, he lost a recruiting-ground, and for this he paid, since the Afghān nobles were not by any means tamed. The visits of Humāyun to Delhi were few and far between, for his presence was constantly required elsewhere, to repress revolts in the provinces, especially in Behār, where the Afghān Farid-ud-din Sher Khān had practically made himself independent. Eventually Humāyun was twice defeated by him, once by treachery at Chonsa, once in fair fight at Kanāuj in 1540, escaping from his pursuers with difficulty. But we have omitted to notice one or two important events connected with Delhi, which had occurred before this.

In A.D. 1534 Humāyun conceived the building of a new fort at Delhi, which he proposed to call Din Panāh, "shelter of the faith," and it was pointed out to him by his courtiers, who were mostly astrologers, that this would be a fortunate year in which to commence the enterprise. He therefore proceeded to Delhi, laid the first brick with his own hands, and then sailed down the Jumna to Agra in a floating palace which he had himself designed.

In 1538 Hindal Mirzā, brother of Humāyun, revolted against him, caused himself to be proclaimed emperor at Agra, and marched to Delhi, presumably there to ascend the throne in due form. Two faithful nobles, however, anticipated his arrival by making forced marches, and held Firozābād against him. Kāmrān, the brother who possessed the Punjāb, came to Hindal's aid, but the stout defence of Fakhr-ud-din made them raise the siege. The two brothers then went to Agra, and Humāyun might have been deposed, had not a common danger, in the shape of Sher Khān, caused all to combine for safety. Kāmrān soon abandoned the confederacy and returned to the Punjāb, so Humāyun moved against Sher Khān alone, but was defeated at Kanāuj.

Pursued hotly, Humāyun reached Delhi on May 25, 1540, but could not remain, and had to march on into the Punjāb, to wander homeless for many a long year, through Sind into Persia, until at length he was able to re-establish a kingdom in Cābul. While in Sind he married, in 1541, Hamida Begam, then only fourteen years of age, and on the 15th of October in the following year there was born to him a son, the great Akbar, at Umarkot, on the confines of the Indian desert. The circumstances of the birth, while the mother was enduring the hardships of a flight, made it necessary to employ foster-mothers, wives of nobles who were accompanying Humāyun. Several monuments at Delhi are connected with the foster-relations of Akbar.

Farid-ud-din, having driven out Humāyun, ascended the throne in 1540 with the title of SHER SHĀH. Although Agra was his capital, he commenced to build a wall round part of Firozābād, adjoining the Purāna Kila of Humāyun; but he cannot have spent many days there, for he was very busy throughout his short reign in conquering Malwa and other countries. He died in 1545 in the trenches before Kalinjar, a fort in Bengal, and was buried at Sasseram. He built caravan-sarāis, at every ten kos distance, all the way from Bengal to the Indus, and had wells dug at each kos; he also caused to be erected "kos minārs," many of which stand to this day, although the old road has been ploughed up, and merged in the fields. To Sher Shāh, also, are attributed the "Kila Kona" Mosque, and the "Sher Mandal," both in Humāyun's Fort.

ISLAM SHĀH, commonly called Salim, now succeeded his father, and, like him, made Agra his capital. In 1546, however, he was at Delhi for a short time, and commenced the construction of the fort of Salimgarh; he also ordered the walls of the Purāna Kila to be rebuilt in lime. In 1551 he undertook an expedition into the Punjāb, and had hardly returned to Delhi when he was informed of the advance of Humāyun, to attempt the recovery of his lost kingdom. Islām set out at once, not waiting for bullocks to draw his artillery, which had to be drawn by hand; so heavy were the guns that a thousand men are said to have been required for each. Of course the roads were then not metalled. Humāyun would not meet him, but retired, and Islām returned from Lahore to Agra, whence he went to Gwalior, a place which he preferred to either Agra or Delhi. He died in A.D. 1553. Besides his other buildings, he erected an intermediate sarāi between every two of his father's, and thus was equally a public benefactor.

On the death of Islām Shāh, his son Firoz Khān was placed on the throne, but he was at once murdered by Mobarez Khān, cousin of Islām, who ascended the throne with the title of Mahomed Adil Shāh, "the just king." He had a minister named Himu, a Hindu of humble origin, who had been a small trader at Rewāri; of him we shall hear again. But now he had to retire with his master into Bengal, before Ibrāhim Sur, brother-in-law of Adil Shāh. Ibrāhim had seized Delhi, and ascended the throne there; but this orthodox coronation was not to save him from deposition, for Sikandar Shāh, nephew of Sher Shāh and Governor of the Punjāb, possessed himself of Delhi, and defeated Ibrāhim at Farah, near Agra. Thus in a few months four kings had, in succession, ascended the throne, and three were alive still, warring amongst themselves, at the beginning of 1555.

Humāyun, finding India weakened by these internecine struggles, made a second attempt to recover the country, and was successful. He invaded the Punjāb, sending his general, Bahrām Khān, ahead, and was himself present at the battle of Sirhind, where he defeated Sikandar's large army. He then advanced to Delhi, and reoccupied the place on July 23, 1555, after a stay of three days in Salimgarh.

The few months which elapsed before his death Humāyun spent, not in vigorous expeditions, but in the apportioning of the provinces amongst his nobles—a dangerous project in days when each man's hand was for himself. Part of his time, also, he spent in the design of a wonderful astrological palace, with radiating halls of different colours, called by the names of the planets. In these audience was to be given, on corresponding days of the week, to the professions under the guidance of those planets. In fact, although not yet an old man, he was probably not quite sane. His death was due to his astrological studies. One evening he was told that Venus ought to be visible, and he determined, if he saw the planet, to promote certain nobles, as it would be fortunate to do so. He accordingly went to the top of the Sher Mandal, from which he could observe the setting sun; as he was descending he heard the muezzin at the Kila Kona Mosque call to prayer. He therefore sat down on the steps until the call should be finished; when he rose again, he slipped and rolled to the bottom, sustaining a severe wound on his temple. Some say that he was stupefied by an over-dose of opium. The wound was the cause of his death on January 24, 1556; his grandfather had died by a similar accident.

Delhi in Moghal Times

JALĀL-UD-DIN MAHOMED AKBAR, son of Humāyun, was away in the Punjāb; the events of the past few years had left many claimants to the throne, and the death of Humāyun had occurred at a singularly inopportune moment. It was therefore determined to conceal the fact of his death, and for seventeen days a eunuch, dressed in the royal robes, appeared at the daily ceremony of public audience, while couriers with despatches hastened to Bahrām Khān, who was with Akbar. At last Akbar was proclaimed, but he was not to obtain the throne unopposed, for Himu, the minister of Adil Shāh, determined to contest his right. He advanced swiftly on Agra, and occupied that place, while Akbar's generals retired to Delhi, but had to abandon the place after sustaining defeat. Himu then assumed the name of Rāja Vikramaditya, and advanced to the historic field of Pānipat with a large army and many elephants. There Akbar and Bahrām Khān engaged him. Himu was wounded in the eye with an arrow, taken prisoner, and put to death by order of Bahrām Khān—an officious action which Akbar resented, but did not dare to notice. Thus the Moghals, for the second time, obtained the Empire of India at Pānipat, and Akbar at once took possession of Delhi.

This emperor did not retain Delhi as his

capital, so, although the city was known as "Takht Dilli," or Royal Delhi, it became almost deserted; the old retainers of Humāyun, however, lived there, and were there buried. The policy of Akbar was one of conciliation of the Hindu princes, whose daughters he sought in marriage, and whom he appointed nobles and generals of his army; consequently the southern capital of Agra was thought by him more suitable.

The emperor, however, in the early part of his reign, paid several visits to Delhi, in order to visit his foster-mother, Māhim Anāgāh, mother of Adham Khān. It was probably due to her influence that he decided there to deprive Bahrām Khān of his office as prime minister, and to assume the reins of government, although he was at that time only eighteen years of age. His foster-mother's influence also obtained for Adham Khān the command of an expedition into Mālwa, where he was successful, but withheld the spoils from the emperor, who said little, but deprived him of employment. Taga Khān, the husband of another foster-mother of Akbar, was in high favour; this caused the jealousy of Adham Khān, who murdered Taga Khān in the audience-chamber. Akbar heard the noise of the scuffle, came out of his chamber, and half drew his sword to kill Adham Khān, but he reflected that such an action would be unbecoming to his dignity, sheathed the sword, and asked sternly the reason for the deed. Adham Khān seized his hands and implored mercy, but Akbar felled him with his fist, and ordered him to be thrown down from the battlements—an operation which had to be twice performed before he expired. Māhim Anāgāh died of grief at the fate of her son, and was buried beside him in the mausoleum which stands on the walls of Old Delhi. Taga Khān was buried near the shrine of Nizām-ud-din Auliā.

Mirzā Aziz Kokaltāsh, the son of Taga Khān, received his honours and most of his appointments, except that of chancellor of the empire; he had a great career, and, although he was sometimes rather insubordinate, Akbar would never punish him severely, saying, "Between him and myself there flows a river of milk." He was Governor, in turn, of Ahmedābād, Guzerāt, and of Mālwa, but in 1594 did not care to stand an inquiry into his administration, and sailed to Mecca. He returned in the following year so disgusted at the extortions he had experienced at that place, that he embraced a new religion of Akbar's. He had previously scoffed at this religion, and this proved a serious matter to him;

Jahāngir, after succeeding his father, was given a letter of Mirzā Aziz, ridiculing Akbar, and deprived him of all his honours and lands, and threw him into prison. In 1608 his rank was restored to him, and he lived until 1624, when he died at the good old age of eighty-five; he was buried in his "hall of sixty-four pillars."

In 1563 Akbar paid another visit to Delhi, and had a narrow escape from assassination there. As he was passing the college of Māhim Anāgāh, opposite the fort of Humāyun, a servant of a rebel noble fitted an arrow to his bow, and pointed it to the sky, as if to shoot at a bird. The emperor's retinue gazed upward, completely off their guard, and the archer turned his arrow against the emperor and let fly, the arrow embedding itself in Akbar's shoulder. The guards at once cut the miscreant down, wounding each other in their haste; the arrow proved not to be poisoned, for the wound quickly healed.

In 1576 Akbar passed through on his way to join an expedition against Cābul, but the sight of a tremendous comet caused him to abandon his intention. He died in 1605, and was buried in a magnificent tomb at Sikandra, near Agra.

Nur-ud-din Jahāngir, the eldest son, succeeded to the throne; his other name was Salim,

WALLS OF SHER SHĀH'S DELHI.

COLLEGE OF MĀHAM ANĀGĀH.

[To face p. 222.

given him by the Chisti saint at Fatehpur Sikri, by the efficacy of whose prayers a son was born to Akbar, and lived, while previous children had died. Delhi still remained a neglected capital, and was given as an estate to Sāyyad Kamāl, the son of a Bokhāra noble, while Jahāngir spent most of his time at Ajmere and Māndu, and other places. He, however, on several occasions visited the city, the first occasion being in 1606, while in pursuit of his son Khusru, who had rebelled and fled to the Punjāb. During his short stay at Delhi, Jahāngir visited the tomb of his grandfather, Humāyun, and the shrine of Nizām-ud-din Auliā, distributing (so he says) a hundred thousand rupees in charity. On his return from Lahore, victorious over his son, he ordered trees to be planted along the high-road, sarāis to be erected and to be provided with baths and reservoirs for fresh water; servants also were appointed to wait on travellers, as in dāk bungalows. As a matter of fact, the sarāis had been built by Sher Shāh and Islām Shāh, but no official notice could be taken of this. Bridges also were built over the streams, among others one of eleven arches near Humāyun's tomb, on the Muttra Road.

In 1615 King James the First sent an embassy to Jahāngir, under Sir Thomas Roe, but the members of this did not proceed as far even as Agra, for the emperor was then at Ajmere and Māndu. A Captain Hawkins, with other merchant-mariners lent out by the East India Company, had previously reached Agra. One of these, William Finch, journeyed, early in 1611, by way of Delhi, to Lahore on business, and has left a journal of his travels, to which reference has been made. Finch was probably the first European to see Delhi; if one of the Jesuits, or Dutchmen, who lived at Agra in Akbar's time, preceded him, we have no record of it. In 1615 a certain Thomas Coryate, who lived very much by his wits at the Court of King James, undertook to walk to the court of the Great Moghal, and actually did so walk, all the way from Aleppo to Agra. The journey took him ten months, and only cost him the small sum of three pounds sterling, of ten shillings of which he was cheated; he must have been the first of those enterprising persons who for a wager have wandered around the globe at the expense of the good-natured. He passed through Delhi, but the only object which attracted his attention was the Pillar of Asoka, which was then still surmounted by the gilded ball and crescent. Later in this same year, Richard Steel and John Crowther passed through on a journey to Ispahān, and have recorded that "the inhabitants are poor and beggarly, by reason of the king's long absence."

In 1618 Jahāngir passed through Delhi on his way to Cashmere; he mentions seeing a species of bird with a peculiar tail. Twenty thousand of these were captured by some Cashmerians, who made a sort of murmuring sound, which had an irresistible attraction for the birds, and they walked into the nets. Perhaps they were pintailed sand-grouse.

In 1623 Prince Khurram, afterwards Shāh Jahān, rebelled against his father, and attempted to take Agra, but, being twice foiled, advanced on Delhi, and halted at Faridābād. Jahāngir was then residing at Delhi, and was at first greatly alarmed, but plucked up courage as reinforcements joined him, and moved out to battle. The two armies met opposite Tughlukābād, and an indecisive engagement followed; but the prince's troops could not be kept together, so he had to flee. The last years of Jahāngir's life were spent in the Punjāb, at Cābul, and in Cashmere, where he was taken ill; he died before he could reach Lahore, to which place his body was taken. He was buried at Shāhdara, on the north bank of the river Rāvi, opposite Lahore.

Prince Khurram was at this time in the Deccan, and Jahāngir had nominated another son to succeed him, but this son was defeated, taken prisoner by Khurram's adherents, and then, as usual, blinded. Until Prince Khurram could arrive, a nephew of his was set up as emperor. When the Prince came, he cruelly had the puppet-king strangled, and removed every possible disputant of the throne. This was a return to methods of barbarism, for which he suffered when he saw his own son do the same to his brothers. He caused himself to be proclaimed emperor at Agra early in 1628, and assumed the titles of ABUL MUZAFFAR SHĀHAB-UD-DIN, SHĀH JAHĀN, SĀHIB-I-KIRĀN SĀNI.

The first few years of his reign were occupied in wars in the Deccan, and the emperor did not return to Agra until the year 1633. Two years previously his favourite sultāna, Arjamund Bānu Begam, had died, and over her grave he ordered to be built the beautiful mausoleum which we have learnt to call the "Tāj Mahāl," a wrong term for it; the natives call it "Tāj Bibi ka Roza," the "Tāj lady's tomb," which is more correct. It seems a pity to destroy the legend that Shāh Jahān was faithful to her memory; but that he was not, for we have noticed at least three mosques at Delhi built by his wives. That he was faithful to her while she lived seems true, and that was a great compliment.

Shāh Jahān now embarked on a programme of building palaces, including the one at Agra; in 1648, he moved into his new palace at Delhi. In the same year he started his city walls, first building them in stone and mud, but afterwards in lime, for the rains soon played havoc with them. He had previously visited Delhi, in 1634, on his way to Cashmere, and passed through again on his return in the following year. Between Delhi and Agra the wife of Dāra Shikoh, his eldest son, presented him with a grandson, and on this occasion of rejoicing he first mounted the wonderful Peacock Throne, which had been seven years in the making.

In 1657 he was seized with a paralytic stroke at Delhi, and was only relieved by copious bleeding. The people were much concerned, and all business was suspended until the bulletins announced his convalescence. He was then moved to Agra by boat, under the superintendence of Dāra Shikoh; but the news of his death had reached the provinces, and each son moved his powerful army towards Agra. Aurangzeb and Murād joined forces, and Dāra, with the king's army, engaged them not far from Agra, but was defeated and had to flee. Aurangzeb imprisoned his father, got rid of Murād by stratagem, and proceeded to Delhi, where he ascended the throne at the Shāhlimār Gardens, in the year 1658; he assumed the title of Alamgir, but was always known as AURANGZEB. Shāh Jahān spent the remaining years of his life at Agra, attended by his daughter Jahanāra, and there he died in 1666. He once asked Aurangzeb to permit him to see his palace at Delhi, and Aurangzeb agreed, on condition only that he would make the journey by water. This the old man refused to do, and his son would not risk the possibility of deposition if his father were allowed to make a progress by land, and thus win over the people. Shāh Jahān was buried by the side of his favourite wife.

Aurangzeb by this time was firmly seated on the throne, for all his brothers and close relatives were either dead or safely in prison. Dāra had been taken prisoner, and brought to Delhi, through the streets of which he was paraded on an elephant; he was then confined at Khizrābād, near Humāyun's tomb. Aurangzeb consulted with some nobles whether he should be allowed to live, and one only proposed the capital penalty, on the ground that he was an apostate from the Mahomedan religion. Aurangzeb, perhaps, remembered that Dāra always stigmatised him as "that bigot," and eagerly seized on the pretext, ordering his execution, which was carried out the same night. The head of Dāra was taken to

Aurangzeb, as evidence of his death, and the hypocrite shed tears over it; it was then buried with Dāra's body, on the platform of Humāyun's tomb.

Aurangzeb spent a considerable time at Delhi, which now resumed its position as the capital city. His sister Roshanāra lived there until her death in 1663, and Jahanāra joined him there after the death of their father. In 1661 there was a dreadful famine in the city, and many of the inhabitants perished, in spite of the exertions of the emperor, who was a careful ruler of his people. But he was too much of a bigot, and oppressed the Hindus, so that the Rājputs revolted in 1680, being joined by the emperor's son with his division of the imperial army, numbering, it is said, five hundred thousand men. Swift retribution followed the revolt, but no measures, however severe, could make the Rājputs submit, and eventually Aurangzeb had to call a truce, to enable him to carry on a war in the Deccan, which he was most anxious to add to his empire. He never succeeded, and died at Ahmadnagar in 1707; there he is buried. From this time onward the fortunes of the Moghals steadily declined, and Delhi shared in their ill-fortune.

On the death of Aurangzeb, his son Muazzim hastened down from Cābul, and engaged his brother Azam, Governor of the Deccan, on the same field, near Agra, where their father had defeated Dāra. Six hundred and fifty thousand men are said to have been engaged on both sides, and the result was a victory for Muazzim, who ascended the throne with the title of Shah Alam Bahādur Shāh. A third brother, Kāmbaksh, endeavoured to wrest the empire from him, but was unsuccessful, and died of his wounds. Bahādur Shāh seems to have done nothing of importance at Delhi, and died in 1710, at Lahore, during an expedition against the Sikhs. His body was brought to Delhi, and buried near the shrine of Kutb-ud-din.

The reign of the next emperor, Jahāndār Shāh, was a short one. He had to fight for his throne with his brothers, and was only successful by the aid of one Zulficar Khān, whom he appointed prime minister and virtual ruler of his dominions, while Jahāndār gave himself up to pleasure. He became completely infatuated with a dancing-girl, and desired to appoint her relatives to all the important posts—a course of conduct which aroused the anger and disgust of two brothers, Sāyyads, named Abdulla Khān and Hasan Khān. These two took up arms against him, and defeated him near Agra, forcing him to fly; but he was captured and put to death, and was buried on the platform of Humāyun's tomb. This was in 1713.

The king-maker Sāyyads then placed on the throne the nephew of the previous king, by name FARUKHSIYAR. He was, somewhat naturally, a mere puppet; when he attempted to rid himself of his keepers, he was taken prisoner, blinded, and put to death. He also was buried at Humāyun's tomb.

One important event of his reign must be recorded. In 1716, Farukhsiyar fell sick; a Scotch surgeon, Gabriel Hamilton, was summoned to attend him, and effected a cure. Asked to state his fee, this noble and disinterested man requested a warrant exempting the East India Company from payment of duty within the emperor's dominions, on consideration of an annual payment in lieu. This implied a recognition of the status of the Company, and gave them grounds for negotiations, which eventually led to important results.

Farukhsiyar was murdered in 1719, and the Sāyyads raised to the throne in quick succession two boys; one of these they murdered, the other died soon after his succession. Both were buried at Humāyun's tomb. The king-makers then placed on the throne MAHOMED SHĀH—disastrous name, for each ruler of that name saw invaders devastate his dominions. The empire now gradually became dismembered. The Governor of the Deccan, Nizām-ul-Mulk, although calling himself a subject, was practically independent at Hyderābād; while the Governor of Oudh set up what was really a separate kingdom at Lucknow. In the second year of his reign, 1720, Mahomed Shāh set out to suppress the Nizām-ul-Mulk, accompanied by Hasan Khān, one of the two Sāyyads; the latter was assassinated near Agra, and Mahomed Shāh, seizing the chance, returned towards Delhi, in order to dispose of the other brother. Abdulla Khān marched against him, but was defeated and taken prisoner near Shergarh, about twenty miles north of Muttra. He was taken to Delhi, and died there of his wounds. Mahomed Shāh was much pressed to revenge on him the murder of his cousin Farukhsiyar, but magnanimously refused to do so, as one brother had already expiated the crime.

In 1737 Mahomed Shāh summoned the Nizām-ul-Mulk to Delhi, nominally to assist him in straightening out the tangled condition of the affairs of the empire, really to disgrace him. The nizām, however, was much too astute, and came with a bodyguard of twenty thousand men, so that Mahomed quailed at carrying out his project.

Mahomed remained under the evil influence of Khān Daurān, the captain-general of the empire, so the Nizām, powerless to interfere, and submitted to insult, returned to the Deccan in a huff. In order to arouse the emperor to a sense of his duties, he arranged a Mahratta raid on the Northern Provinces, of which Mahomed took no notice, until the enemy, under Bāji Rāo, arrived at the temple of Kālikā, six miles from Delhi, where a fair was going on. They defeated the king's troops, but were bought out by Saādat Khān, Nawāb of Oudh. Again the Nizām was summoned, again he was treated with disrespect and his counsel was laughed at, so he entered into negotiations with Saādat Khān, and the two sent a joint letter to Kuli Khān, Nādir Shāh of Persia, asking him to give the emperor a lesson. He was nothing loth, and set out in the latter part of 1738 with an army of thirty-six thousand horse; the army of Mahomed Shāh, after one false start, marched out of Delhi and camped on the plains of Karnāl. Nādir Shāh met with very little opposition, for the Subahdārs of Peshawar and of Lahore had been advised by the Nizām not to fight seriously, so the two armies soon came face to face, and for some days sat down opposite each other. Then a plundering raid developed unexpectedly into a battle, in which the troops of Mahomed Shāh, who were estimated at two hundred thousand strong, received a defeat, but were not driven from the camp.

After some days of perplexity and wavering counsel, Mahomed, afraid of the intrigues of the Nizām, who was bargaining with the enemy, surrendered himself to Nādir Shāh, and was received with the respect due to a king. He was, however, reproached with his inattention to the affairs of his state and with his want of generalship, and was informed that the empire would not be taken from him, but that Delhi would be occupied until an indemnity was paid. On March 9, 1739, Nādir Shāh, preceded by Mahomed Shāh, entered Delhi, and took up his quarters in the palace, Mahomed contenting himself with the Shāh Burj, while the invader occupied the main apartments. Strict orders were given that the inhabitants were not to be molested, but on the evening of the 10th a scuffle was started by some grain-sellers at Pahārganj, and a report was spread that Nādir Shāh had been killed. A riot quickly developed, and Nādir Shāh, highly incensed, proceeded on the following morning to quell it. As he entered the Golden Mosque of Roshan-ud-daula, in the Chāndni Chouk, a musket was fired at him, and the ball narrowly missed. He gave orders at once for a general massacre. From the

Jewellers' Bāzār to the old Idgāh, and from the "Chittli" tomb (near the Jāma Masjid) to the Mithāi Bridge in the Teliwāra Mandi, slaughter and fire and pillage raged in a most barbarous manner, from eight in the morning until three in the afternoon. Then Mahomed Shāh sent an envoy to make personal intercession, and the slaughter was stopped, after over a hundred thousand people had been killed, many of whom were perfectly innocent men, women, and children. On the 13th a second, but smaller, massacre succeeded a second riot, and the work of clearing the dead bodies, piled in heaps in the streets, took several days. For many years afterwards the quarter near the Golden Mosque remained almost deserted, so terrible was the memory of this event, which is commemorated by the name, "Khuni Darwāza," given to the gate near which the massacre commenced.

Many days were spent in settling the details of the ransom to be exacted from the city, four crores of rupees (four millions sterling) being demanded. Mahomed Shāh was reinstated and advised to beware of the Nizām, and a marriage took place between the son of Nādir Shāh and a great-granddaughter of Aurangzeb, the rejoicings at which must have been somewhat forced. At length, on the 5th of May, Nādir Shāh left Delhi for the Shāhlimār Gardens, the first stage on his return to Persia. The total value of the plunder has been estimated at eighty crores of rupees, and the famous Peacock Throne was carried off; the territory west of the Indus was ceded, and two hundred thousand people altogether are said to have lost their lives.

Heavily mulcted as the inhabitants of Delhi had been, it must have been with feelings of relief that they saw the departure of the invader; his efforts to awake Mahomed Shāh to a better judgment cannot have been more acceptable than the expedition of the Powers to Pekin, to help the Chinese rulers against the "Boxers," can have been to the Chinese nation. But the lesson was of little use to Mahomed Shāh. Saādat Khān of Oudh had died, on the 9th of March, of an illness which looked uncommonly like the effects of poison, and the Nizām had returned to the Deccan and become independent. There is a story that both these nobles were bitterly upbraided by Nādir Shāh for their unpatriotic conduct in calling him in, that they retired from the audience and agreed to take poison, but that the Nizām took a harmless draught and pretended to die, coming to life again when Saādat Khān was reported to have really carried out his part of the compact.

Kamr-ud-din, a trusty adherent of the Nizām, was now reappointed prime minister, but he was not able to stop the falling off of the limbs of the decaying empire—Bengal, Behar, Orissa, and Rohilkand all becoming independent. The emperor was able actually to defeat the rebel who had possessed himself of the last-named province, but could not bring back the country under his rule. Then came another invasion from the north, under Ahmad Khān Abdāli, the leader of the Durāni Afghāns. Strange to say, the Moghal army was able to defeat him. One of the generals of that army was Mansur Ali Khān, Safdar Jang, but he soon retired, and it was through no fault of his that the victory was won. Unfortunately, during the action the prime minister was killed in his tent, by a cannon-ball, while at prayer. The emperor was deeply attached to him, and grieved so greatly over his loss that he fell down in a fit and expired. He had reigned twenty-nine years, and died in 1747. His tomb is in one of the marble enclosures near the shrine of Khwāja Nizām-ud-din Auliā.

The observatory, which now goes by the grotesque name of "Jantar Mantar," was constructed during the reign of this emperor, and his wife, Kudsia Begam, made the garden outside the Cashmere Gate which is called by her name.

Mahomed Shāh was succeeded by his son, Ahmad Shāh, and the office of prime minister was assumed by Safdar Jang, the office being made hereditary in the Oudh family. The old Nizām of Hyderābād died at the commencement of this reign, at the age of a hundred and three. Now the Rohillas again revolted, and Safdar Jang, the "disperser of the battle ranks," called in the aid of Hindus, summoning the Mahrattas and the Jāts. There was no way of paying for their services, except to assign them the revenues of the conquered province, so the glory still further departed. Then, in 1749, the Durāni chieftain again appeared on the scene; the Hindu auxiliaries were summoned to Delhi to oppose him, but the emperor bought him off by the cession of the provinces of Lahore and Multān. The presence of the Hindu mercenaries at Delhi was dangerous, for they were clamorous for pay, and might at any moment seize the city; so they were sent off to the Deccan to aid the son of the old Nizām to recover for himself that province, which had been usurped by his brother. There was left behind a grandson of the Nizām, named Ghāzi-ud-din, and this young man worthily upheld the party, to which he belonged, against the Oudh faction, at the head of which was Safdar Jang, the minister. Delhi saw almost daily scuffles between these Montagus and Capulets, which eventually resulted in the rise of the Deccan party to power. In 1751 Safdar Jang revolted, and called to his aid the Bhartpur Jāts, under Suraj Mal; Ghāzi-ud-din bravely defended Delhi against them for five months, in 1753. He eventually defeated the Jāts, in his turn calling on the Mahrattas under Holkar to complete the suppression of that tribe. Now the emperor must needs take a hand in a game which he did not in the least understand, and marched towards Bhartpur nominally to aid the young Ghāzi, who was besieging that place, really to betray him. A letter from Ahmad Shāh to Suraj Mal unfortunately fell into the hands of Ghāzi-ud-din; Holkar, the ally of the latter, attacked, took, and plundered the emperor's camp; Ahmad Shāh fled to Delhi, to be followed and invested by Ghāzi, to whom he had to open the gates. A council of nobles inquired into the emperor's conduct in intriguing against "his own friends," and advised his deposition, which was at once carried out. But it will be remembered that deposed monarchs had previously been able to regain their kingdom, unless rendered unfit to rule, and that was effected by blinding. This operation was carried out in one of two ways: the eyes could be cut by a lancet, which had a disfiguring effect, or could be seared by a red-hot wire pencil. Which method was adopted in this case does not matter, but blinded the emperor was, and consigned to the state prison at Salimgarh. He disappears from history, and the date of his death is not known, nor the place of his burial, although one account places it near the Kadam Sharif.

The new emperor was the son of Jahāndār Shāh, and ascended the throne with the title of ALAMGIR SANI, the "second conqueror of the world." As a matter of fact, he was not even master of his capital; Ghāzi-ud-din was the virtual ruler without fear of a rival, for Safdar Jang died at this time, A.D. 1754. The empire had been reduced to a few districts around Delhi, the Punjāb was gone, the Deccan and Oudh were separate kingdoms, and practically all the rest of India belonged to the Mahrattas, except the gradually increasing territories of the Honourable East India Company. The battle of Plassey was fought in the fourth year of Alamgir's reign, on June 23, 1757.

Alamgir was now foolish enough to intrigue against his master, and thought he saw a good way to undermine the power of Ghāzi by calling in the Durāni, who indeed did not require much invitation, for he had been greatly incensed by a successful raid of Ghāzi-ud-din on Lahore. When Ahmad Khān arrived within twenty miles of Delhi, Ghāzi moved out against him, but the intrigues of Alamgir caused the desertion of a great part of his troops, whereupon Ghāzi made the most of his personality to ingratiate himself with the invader, succeeding so well that he at once got into great favour with him. Ahmad Khān entered Delhi on January 20, 1757, and assumed the government, extorting money from the unhappy people, and inflicting on them indignities which must have almost made them sigh for Nādir Shāh. After a stay of two months Ahmad Khān proceeded to Muttra to sack that place, and lay waste the Jāt territories, leaving Ghāzi-ud-din as powerful as ever in Delhi, and Alamgir, as we may suppose, deeply regretting his arrant folly, his failure in intrigue, and the enmity which he had aroused in Ghāzi's breast. That individual had in him a vein of great cruelty which overshadowed his better nature, and he now commenced a general oppression, backing his power by the employment of a horde of Mahratta mercenaries, the payment of whom came from his unfortunate enemies in the state.

In 1759 Ahmad Khān Abdāli again invaded the country, and Ghāzi did not feel at all comfortable at his approach; he determined to rid himself of Alamgir before his power to do so vanished. He therefore caused it to be reported to the king that a holy man had taken up his quarters in the Kotila of Firoze Shāh; it was suggested that Alamgir should visit him there. The king had a partiality for religious mendicants, and readily agreed, but there awaited him only an assassin, who killed him with his dagger, cut off his head, and threw the headless trunk on to the river sands below, whence it was taken and buried on the platform of Humāyun's tomb. The Durāni chieftain at once moved on Delhi, Ghāzi-ud-din had to flee, and eventually he was deported to Mecca, in 1780, by the British police of Surat. He returned and died in retirement about 1800.

Not finding any one else to punish, Ahmad Khān visited the retribution of the crime on the innocent inhabitants of Delhi, now almost deserted; he ordered a seven days' slaughter, sacked the city, and then, leaving a garrison in the palace, retired to Anupshahr.

The Mahrattas and the Jāts now combined to drive out the Mahomedans and establish Hindu rule. After sustaining one defeat by the Durānis they forced them to retire, and easily took possession of Delhi, proceeding to strip the palace of all that was valuable, and that had been left by

Nādir Shāh and by Ahmad Khān Abdāli. This was not much, for the latter had gleaned well; but they took the silver ceiling of the Diwān Khās, and such precious stones as they were able to gouge out of the pillars. They then advanced to Pānipat with a vast army—fifty-five thousand good cavalry (an arm in which they excelled), a large train of artillery, and fifteen thousand French-trained infantry, supplemented by perhaps two hundred thousand irregulars. Against this formidable force Ahmad Khān was able to place about fifty thousand cavalry, a small train of artillery, and some forty thousand Indian—recruited infantry; but the discipline of his army was better, and the Mahrattas were subjected to a blockade for the space of two months. Fear of famine at last brought on the action; but the Jāts deserted, Holkar left the field, and a colossal massacre of the remaining Mahrattas took place in the village of Pānipat. So on January 6, 1761, at the third battle of Pānipat, another dream of Hindu rule faded away, entirely through a lack of cohesion, brought about by too selfish and constant consideration of private interests. No chief would allow his forces to engage seriously, for he might be ruined, while others drew off their troops in order to retain their territories.

Ahmad Khān once again occupied Delhi, but soon retired after sending his salutations to Ali Gohar, the heir-apparent, who had previously fled from Delhi to Lucknow, fearing, and with good reason, the designs of Ghāzi-ud-din upon his life.

Shāh Ālam, as the new king had termed himself on receiving the news of the assassination of his father, did not reach Delhi until ten years later, after having kept up some sort of a court at Allāhābād, with the aid of an annual subsidy of twenty-six lakhs of rupees from the East India Company. His son, Mirzā (or Prince) Jiwan Bakht was meanwhile, by permission of the Mahrattas, regent at Delhi over a very small territory. At the end of 1763 Suraj Mal, the Jāt chief, after occupying Agra, and seating himself on the throne of the Moghals (which at once cracked), advanced to Ghāzi-ud-din Nagar, eighteen miles from Delhi, but was taken by surprise and killed. The sight of his head on a lance was sufficient for the discomfiture of his troops when they arrived too late. His son then allied himself with Malhar Rāo Holkar, and was able to besiege Delhi for three months, until Holkar came to an understanding with their enemy, suddenly left him, and the siege was raised. In 1767 the Sikhs threatened Delhi.

The prime minister was then Najib-ud-daulah, a Rohilla, who called in the Durāni once more, but he did not on this occasion approach nearer than Pānipat, and then retired from Hindustān for ever. The Sikhs after this became too strong, and kept the Afghāns within their borders.

In 1770 Najib-ud-daulah died, and was succeeded in his post of wazir by his son, Zabitā Khān; but the Mahrattas drove him out, and in the following year Shāh Ālam, with a small army, returned to Delhi. His troops were commanded by a scion of the Persian royal family, Mirzā Najaf Khān, of whom we shall hear more. Shāh Ālam found a Mahratta army of thirty thousand men at Delhi, but by agreement they acquiesced in his entry on Christmas Day, 1771; he had also the countenance of the East India Company, and had been escorted to the borders of his nominal territory by a British force. The Mahrattas now pursued Zabitā Khān into Rohilkand, his family and treasure fell into their hands, and his son, Ghulām Kādir, was presented to Shāh Ālam, who took a serpent into his bosom.

Zabitā Khān now intrigued with the Mahrattas for his reinstatement as prime minister, and they supported his cause, their army advancing on Delhi. The king's troops met them at Badarpur, on the Muttra Road, near Tughlukābād, and a series of skirmishes ensued, as the result of which the imperial force had to retire to Humāyun's tomb, and then to Dariāganj. The king threw over Najaf Khān, and accepted Zabitā Khān as his minister. The former fortified himself in a sarāi outside the Cābul Gate, but seeing no hope, put on his armour and rode out, as he thought, to his death. Instead, he was respectfully received, and escorted in safety to the Mahratta camp. Why? Because it did not suit them to dispose of a man of such influence, although they had but a few days previously been the instruments of his disgrace. Such a complete change of policy is difficult to understand, but that is just what so often happened—slight incidents or further discussion causing great changes of policy, it might be on two successive days. It is therefore impossible to detail fully the events of the next few years, but some important events may be briefly noticed.

In 1775 the Jāt power was broken by Najaf Khān at the battle of Barsāna, and this intrepid noble took the strong fortress of Dig in the following year. In 1777 he engaged the Rohillas, under Zabitā Khān, at Pānipat; the action was indecisive, but a compact, ratified by marriages, brought peace. In 1779 he signally defeated the Sikhs at Meerut, and thus was successful in three campaigns against the enemies of his master. But death overtook him in 1782, and removed the last prop of the decayed trunk of the Moghal empire; he was buried at Aliganj, near Safdar Jang's tomb. The year following his death was one of fearful famine.

In 1785 Zabitā Khān died, and Ghulām Kādir succeeded to his estates. In the same year Shāh Ālam decided to entrust himself to the Mahrattas, under Scindia, who placed a garrison in the palace at Delhi, and was called the "Patel." Ghulām Kādir, however, considered himself sufficiently strong to measure swords with the Mahrattas, and to demand a high post in the state. In 1787 he advanced on Delhi, and encamped at Shāhdara, opposite the palace, the garrison of which opened fire on him from the guns mounted on the walls. Ghulām Kādir was not slow to reply, using, at the same time, that still more effective weapon, money, to lessen the resistance; in the result the Moghals deserted to him, and the Mahrattas evacuated the city. Ghulām Kādir was accorded an audience by Shāh Ālam, and was naturally asked what he meant by firing on the palace. He ascribed his action to his zeal, and protested his loyalty, applying for the patent of Amir-ul-Umra, and retiring. The patent not being forthcoming, he entered the palace three days afterwards and took up his quarters in the house usually ascribed to that functionary. What Shāh Ālam would have done cannot be imagined, had not the Begam Samru of Sardhāna hastened to his aid, and forced Ghulām Kādir to retire across the river. Fresh troops now arrived under a Rewāri noble, and Shāh Ālam melted down his plate to pay others, so that a considerable force was got together to oppose Ghulām Kādir, who started a second cannonade, some of the balls hitting the Diwān Khās. A truce, however, was patched up and Ghulām went off to Aligarh, and on to Agra.

At the beginning of 1788 Shāh Ālam, excited by the unusual sight of an army under his orders, actually undertook an expedition, which had one small triumph, and was then abandoned. Ghulām Kādir and his ally were now defeated by the Mahrattas at Agra, and the former again appeared before Delhi, at Shāhdara; he had another interview with Shāh Ālam, but retired on the arrival of a small Mahratta force. Again was the palace bombarded, again the Moghal soldiery was bought over, and again the Hindus withdrew. Ghulām Kādir presented himself for another interview, and entered the palace with a small body of troops;

he was given a "khilat," or dress of honour, and a richly jewelled shield with the office of prime minister, swearing fealty on the Korān. At a subsequent audience he demanded pay for his troops, and assumed a pretence of anger at the refusal; he disarmed the old king, ordered him into arrest, took a royal prisoner from the Salimgarh prison and placed him on the throne, from which he ordered Shāh Ālam to descend. He then proceeded to ill-treat the old man and the ladies of his family, whom he stripped of their jewellery; he even lounged on the throne beside the wretched puppet whom he had set up, and puffed smoke into his face. Deeds like this were naturally regarded with horror by the people, and the name of Ghulām Kādir still stands for all that is vile; but worse was to come.

The ruffian ordered Shāh Ālam to be brought into the Diwān Khās, and asked him once more to give up the secret of his treasure-house; what could the unfortunate king do but protest that there was no treasure? This must have been perfectly true, for we have seen that, not long before, he had melted down his plate. More words passed, until Shāh Ālam, losing all patience, dared his tormentor to do his worst; whereupon the wretch leaped from the throne, threw him to the ground, and with his own dagger struck out one eye, the attendant Rohillas depriving the other of sight. "What dost thou see?" then asked the traitor. "I see only the holy Korān between you and me," replied Shāh Ālam, with wonderful dignity, referring to the oath of fealty sworn by the perjured scoundrel. He was then removed to the prison of Salimgarh.

Nothing perhaps indicates more clearly the decadence of Mahomedan rule at this period than the fact that a blind man was still recognized as king, for in the course of the history of Delhi we have often seen the contrary. Before, however, proceeding to notice the incidents of the remaining years of Shāh Ālam, let us follow Ghulām Kādir to his well-merited fate.

The news of the awful deed did not at once leak out, but before long the citizens began to leave the city in horror, and the Mahrattas soon appeared again on the scene. Nevertheless Ghulām continued to occupy the palace, although deserted by his former ally, until a considerable army was collected against him before the walls of Delhi. He then blew up a powder-magazine in the palace, emerged at night from the gate of Salimgarh, and joined his troops encamped at Shāhdara. The Mahrattas reoccupied the palace, and were able to extinguish the flames before much damage had been done; the blind king was released, but Ghulām Kādir was not pursued for some days. At length considerable reinforcements arrived, and the ruffian was invested in the fort of Meerut, whence he escaped alone, with such of his plunder as he could carry on his horse. Riding in the dead of night, his horse fell into a "well-run," the inclined way by which the bullocks draw up the leather water-bag. His horse made off, but he was stunned by the fall; in the morning he was taken prisoner, and eventually despatched to Scindia's camp at Muttra. There he was mounted on a donkey, with his face to the tail, and sent round the bāzār; when he abused his guards, his tongue was torn out. Then he was blinded, his nose, ears, hands, and feet were cut off, and in this miserable condition he was sent to Shāh Ālam. But his guards grew tired of carrying him along, and hanged him head downwards on a tree; thus he died. There is a weird story of a black dog, which licked the blood as it dropped from his corpse until both dog and corpse mysteriously disappeared; there seems little reason to suppose that his body was buried at the shrine of Kutb-ud-din, as has been stated by the guardians. Whether he was really responsible for the firing of the cannon-ball which has marked the Iron Pillar must also be doubtful; but any bad act is ascribed to him, just as mutilations of Hindu shrines are ascribed to Aurangzeb, and those of English churches to Cromwell.

The re-enthronement of the blind king was carried out with a certain amount of display at the beginning of 1789, but he was only a pensioner of the Mahrattas, with an income of nine lakhs of rupees (not always paid); the East India Company also allowed him a monthly allowance of two thousand rupees. His only other revenue was derived from occasional "nazrs," or tributary offerings, which even British officers had to give, receiving in return cheap "khilats," or dresses of honour, made of sprigged muslin. He was left in peace for many years, for Mādhāji Scindia of Gwalior, the Patel of the palace, had a splendid army under his French general De Boigne, and there was no one to dispute Delhi with him. Interesting as are the events of this period, full of the wild adventures of the European leaders of the Mahratta forces, there is little to record of Delhi itself.

CHAPTER X

DELHI UNDER "JOHN COMPANY"

Battle of Delhi—Lord Lake's conquest—Siege of Delhi by Holkar—Shāh Ālam a pensioner—Akbar Shāh—British residents—Bahādur Shāh—The succession question.

THERE now appeared on the horizon the forces of another nation; the Honourable East India Company, although a private firm, so to say, by whose license alone Englishmen were permitted to carry on trade in India, had been by now submitted to state control, and was the representative of the British nation. Between their territories and those nominally under the sway of the Moghal king there was nothing but an imaginary frontier, insufficient to hold back those who had the power, and could not be expected for ever to refrain from using it. The Mahratta confederacy was not so stable that treaties were sufficient to enable the two powers to live in concord. "It was either they or we," as Hodson said on another occasion; and the result we know. It is unnecessary to enter into the political causes—the detachment of Scindia from Mahratta headquarters at Poona, the French war in Europe, the presence of many French officers in Scindia's army; all these factors had more or less weight, and gave a certain amount of pretext. The ruling factor, however, was the Company's army, and no Mahomedan or Hindu ruler, with such a force at his disposal, would have hesitated for one moment to widen the confines of his territory.

On September 11, 1803, after a rapid advance, General Lake appeared before Delhi, near the village of Patparganj, east of the Jumna, on plains at that season flooded with water; there the Mahratta garrison of nineteen thousand men opposed him. The British force consisted of H.M. 27th Dragoons, and 76th Foot, two regiments of native cavalry, and seven of native infantry, or four thousand nine hundred men in all. It was relatively small, but the troops were excellent, the general capable, and the result of a long action from 3 a.m. to 7 p.m. was the complete rout of the Mahrattas. On the 14th of September (a significant date in 1857) the British force entered Delhi. Two days later General Lake had an interview with the poor old blind king in the Diwān Khās, receiving from him high-sounding titles and the insignia of a high noble of the now imaginary Moghal empire. He was termed Samsam-ud-daula, Ashgāh-ul-Mulk, Khān Daurān, General Gerard Lake Bahādur, Fateh Jang. Colonel Ochterlony, deputy Adjutant-General of the Company's troops, was appointed Resident at Delhi. As a special distinction, the Governor-General presented an honorary colour to each regiment which had been engaged in the battle.

The forces of Scindia had been disposed of by the battle; but there was yet another Mahratta chieftain to be reckoned with, Jaswant Rāo Holkar. In 1804 he defeated a British force under Colonel Monson, and no other force could be put into the field against him immediately, for it was the rainy season. He advanced to Muttra, abandoned to him by a force of four battalions and two cavalry regiments, and then marched on Delhi with his whole army, which consisted of seventy thousand men and one hundred and thirty guns. On the way he caused to be strangled behind a screen, while his chiefs were being entertained to a banquet, a British soldier, whom he had taken prisoner.

The garrison of Delhi was hastily reinforced; it then consisted of two battalions and four companies of Sepoys (but not a single European company), two regiments of irregular horse, some four hundred tilungas of Scindia's old army, and a corps of najibs, or matchlock men. The old walls of Shāh Jahān were crumbling into ruins, in many places there was no parapet, no ditch had yet been made, and houses permitted an enemy to advance right up to the walls. The inhabitants were scarcely friendly, the palace retainers decidedly unfriendly, and eight companies of the small force had to be detached to garrison the palace. The resident was Colonel Ochterlony; the military commander, Colonel Burn, who had been summoned, with his battalion, from Sahārunpur.

The available troops were drawn out three miles on the Muttra road, and soon prisoners of Colonel Monson's detachment, shockingly mutilated, announced the near approach of the enemy, on hearing of which the irregular cavalry and the najibs either deserted or mutinied. They met with prompt punishment, nine of the ringleaders being blown from a gun; but it was evident that their assistance was not to be counted on. Not one of the regular Sepoys showed a bad spirit, but they were few in number to receive the attack of the formidable Mahratta force, which arrived on the 7th of October, and quickly drove the defenders within the walls. At this juncture the resident received

AJMERE GATE.

TURKMĀN GATE.

[*To face p.* 257.

a letter from the commander-in-chief, ordering the troops to defend the palace only until he could collect an army to relieve the place. Colonel Burn, however, took the responsibility of refusing to listen to orders which had not been sent to himself, and turned a deaf ear to the instructions of the resident, who was junior to himself in the army. He decided to defend the outer walls to the last.

The enemy's artillery being placed in batteries soon made numerous breaches in the shaky old walls; his point of attack was the tower at the south-east angle, then called the "Nila Burj," now improved into the Wellesley Bastion. The rotten wall came down in large masses, and a breach was formed nearly a hundred yards long, but an earthwork was made in rear, and was repaired as fast as it was damaged by the heavy fire. An attempt to storm was repulsed, and gradually the defences at this point were made so strong as to relieve anxiety. A successful sortie against the enemy's batteries, on the night of the 10th of October, made him turn his eyes to another point of attack. The Ajmere Gate, and the curtain between that gate and the Turkmān Gate, were now bombarded, but similar measures of defence resisted all attempts to enter the city; after a final assault on the 14th, the

Mahrattas retired towards Rewāri, three days before the commander-in-chief, with a relieving force from Agra, reached Delhi. Had the enemy attacked at several points simultaneously in the long enceinte the place must have fallen; but that does not detract from this most gallant defence.

In 1805 it was settled that Shāh Ālam should receive a monthly allowance from the East India Company of sixty thousand rupees, that other payments should be made to his relatives, amounting to an additional thirty thousand rupees per mensem, while a certain amount of land was assigned to him for the enjoyment of the revenues. Further, a sum of ten thousand rupees annually was to be paid to him on the occasion of certain festivals; no sentences of death passed on persons living within the city or the assigned territory were to be carried out without his sanction. This was all that remained to the Moghal "emperor," his rights to be called such not being recognized.

In 1806 Shāh Ālam died, and was buried in the royal enclosure, near the shrine of Kutb-ud-din. He was succeeded by his son, Akbar Shah II., whose name recalls memories of a great emperor, but who had still less power than his father had enjoyed, if only for brief intervals. The events of his reign are only of interest so far as they are concerned with British administration. In 1808 his son Mirzā Jahāngir fired a pistol at the British resident, Mr. Archibald Seton, and was removed to Allāhābād, to drink away his life with copious draughts of cherry-brandy. In 1809 the monthly allowances to the king and his family were increased to one lakh of rupees, and perhaps it was this accession of wealth which made him erect in that year the little balcony jutting out of the Musamman Burj. About this time the remodelling of the walls was in full swing, for in 1811 the college of Ghāzi-ud-din, near the Ajmere Gate, was included within an outwork. In 1820, when Sir David Ochterlony, first of the officers of the Company's Army to receive the distinction of K.C.B., had returned as resident, the canal of Ali Mardān Khān was cleared by Lieutenant Rodney Blane, and water again ran through the streets of Delhi, to the great delight of the inhabitants. In 1829 St. James's Church was commenced. In 1832 Delhi was included in the North-Western Provinces. In the same year Mr. William Fraser was appointed agent to the governor-general, and on March 22, 1835, he was murdered, as has been elsewhere described; in the following October the Nāwab of Firozpur was hanged for complicity in the act On the death of Mr. Fraser, Mr.

Thomas Theophilus Metcalfe, who had been assistant-resident, collector, and judge, was appointed agent to the governor-general; he remained in this appointment until his death, establishing his residence at Delhi, and sending to England for all his possessions, including his library, with which he adorned his magnificent mansion. In 1845 Mr. Metcalfe became Sir Thomas, the baronetcy devolving on him through the elevation of Sir Charles Metcalfe to a peerage; he also had been Resident of Delhi. Their father, the first baronet, had been one of the directors of the Honourable East India Company.

In 1837 Akbar Shāh died, and was buried next to his father. There now ascended the throne of Delhi the last of the Moghals, Bahādur Shāh, in the same year as our Queen Victoria came to the throne. The desirability of continuing for ever the succession to a kingdom, which was entirely nominal, was a matter which could not fail to be constantly before the minds of successive governors-general, and when the heir-apparent died in 1849 the question was raised by Lord Dalhousie. A committee was appointed to consider the question, and included the new heir-apparent, Fakhr-ud-din, who was willing to agree to terms by which, on the death of the old king, he was to retire to the Kutb with only the externals of royalty; a document to this effect was therefore drawn up, signed, and sealed in 1850. The principal queen, Zinat Mahal, endeavoured to get the old king to favour her son, Jiwan Bakht, for the succession, and to this he agreed, but was unable to move the Government from their decision. She therefore determined on revenge. Sir Thomas Metcalfe died on November 3, 1853, of symptoms of vegetable poison, supposed by some to have been administered at her instigation. On July 10, 1856, Fakhr-ud-din also died of poison, and Lord Canning had the question to decide afresh. He caused Mirzā Mahomed Korāsh to be recognized as heir, but this prince was informed that, after the old king's death, he would only be styled "shāhzāda," or king's son, and would be given the reduced pension of fifteen thousand rupees per mensem; Zinat Mahal's intrigues, therefore, were again fruitless. And so the line of the Moghal emperors would have quietly come to an end, had not the Fatal Sisters decided otherwise, and Atropos, with her shears, grimly cut the long thread of the Moghal dynasty in a manner which no one could have expected.

CHAPTER XI

THE MUTINY OF 1857, AND THE SIEGE

Outbreak at Meerut—The mutineers at Delhi—Defence of the magazine—The flight—Advance of the avenging army—Battle of Ghāzi-ud-din Nagar—Battle of Badli-ki-Sarāi—Events of the siege—Arrival of the siege train in September—Siege batteries—The assault—Fighting in the city—The city re-taken—Capture of the king.

Plan of the Siege-Works, p. 294.

On the 10th of May, 1857, the Sepoys at Meerut mutinied, shot their officers, and started in a wild rush for Delhi, leaving the work of murder and outrage to be carried on by the scoundrels, who were the hangers-on of every British cantonment. The immediate cause of the mutiny had been the sentencing of eighty-five troopers of the 3rd Regular Bengal Light Cavalry to considerable terms of imprisonment, owing to their refusal to handle cartridges which for years they had used without the slightest protest. This was the work of agitators, who had represented that the cartridges were prepared in a manner designed to take away the caste of Hindus, and to defile Mahomedans; the circumstances are well known, and will not be entered into here. The tempers of their comrades were aroused by the spectacle of the handing over of the convicted troopers to the civil authorities, and by the riveting on of fetters before their eyes, so that it only required a few taunts to arouse them to mutiny. They should have been hotly pursued in their flight by the European troops of the garrison, but the general would not consent; he was afterwards removed from his command. His inaction had terrible results, both for the European population of Delhi and for the British throughout the country; in a moment British prestige vanished, mob law became paramount in the districts around Delhi, the city was occupied by an army of rebel soldiers of the Company's forces, and the question arose whether the British might not be driven into the sea. It was a force of British and loyal native troops, drawn from the Punjāb at great peril to the security of that province, which, without the aid of a single soldier from England, recovered Delhi, broke the back of the rebellion, and lent their aid to the Relief of Lucknow, which has, perhaps, obtained greater fame than the Siege of Delhi.

At Delhi, on the morning of the 11th of May

there was no sign of the coming storm; the magistrates attended court at six in the morning, as was usual during the hot weather, and business was proceeding. Suddenly a report was brought in that rebel troopers had arrived from Meerut, that the toll-house at the far end of the bridge of boats was in flames, and that the Calcutta Gate had been closed against the mutineers. Off went the head magistrate to the cantonments behind the Ridge, to request assistance from the brigadier, who at once ordered down the 54th regiment of Bengal native infantry and two guns to deal with any riot that might arise. There were no European troops in Delhi at all, for the place was considered unhealthy for them, and the authorities had easily deferred to a request of the King of Delhi that none should be stationed there.

Nearly all the principal civil authorities now proceeded to the Calcutta Gate of the city, in order to interview the rebels; they were accompanied by the captain of the Palace Guard, who lived over the Lahore Gate of the palace. But the party was attacked by rebel troopers, who had effected an entrance into the city by the Rājghāt Gate, below the palace; after the encounter they retreated to the Lahore Gate of the palace, where they were massacred by the king's retainers. With them perished the Chaplain of Delhi, his daughter, and a lady friend of hers, who were staying there on a visit.

Meanwhile, the 54th Bengal Native Infantry had marched down to the Cashmere Gate, and through the enclosure, in which was posted the main guard, drawn from the 38th Bengal Light Infantry. The colonel was riding at the head, the officers seem to have been accompanying him as he rode. They were suddenly charged by some of the Meerut troopers, and the colonel, four other officers, and the European sergeant-major, were cut down, all the last five being killed; the other officers and the regimental surgeon had to fly for their lives. Their men did not attempt to defend them, but it is fair to state that the muskets were not loaded. The regiment then went over to the mutineers.

It was now about nine o'clock, and until four in the afternoon all was fairly quiet in the civil lines and cantonments. Small bodies of troops were moved backwards and forwards between the Cashmere Gate and cantonments, but did not proceed into the city to quell the riot. Meanwhile, the Europeans and others, including a number of clerks and pensioners, who lived in Dariāganj, were the helpless prey of the scum of the city, who were not slow to take advantage of the arrival of the rebels; whole families were massacred. Such as were taken prisoners were not allowed to live, being put to death after five days, in the court of the Nakkār Khāna, near a small cistern under a tree.

The officer in charge of the arsenal, Lieutenant George Willoughby, had only a few conductors and non-commissioned officers of the Ordnance Department with him, if we except a guard of native infantry, who were rebels at heart. He soon saw that, without help from Meerut (which all confidently expected), his charge, with stores of ammunition and a whole park of artillery, must fall into the hands of the rebels. He therefore arranged some light guns in positions from which they might be served with the greatest effect against an attack, and, as a last resort, saw that trains of gunpowder were laid to the magazines, so as to blow them up if it were necessary. Arms were issued to the native artificers and lascars, but they were not the men to use them, and escaped at the first opportunity, so that the whole defence devolved on nine resolute Europeans. All these preparations took some little time, but a respite was afforded by the fact that the palace people were looking towards Meerut before committing themselves too far; it was only on the return of a camel sowar,

CASHMERE GATE.

REMAINS OF MAIN GUARD ENCLOSURE.

[*To face p.* 267.

with the intelligence that no British troops were pursuing, that the attack was ordered. When it came the defence could not last long; the attackers were often swept from the walls, but some of the defenders were wounded; no cloud of dust arose on the Meerut Road, all hope of succour was gone. So the signal was given, the trains were fired, and one of the magazines went up into the air, carrying with it a number of the attackers and shaking the whole city.

At the sound of the explosion the Sepoys of the main guard at the Cashmere Gate became restive, and mutiny developed quickly in cantonments. The officers and ladies, who had taken refuge at the Cashmere Gate (most of these were residents in this quarter of the city) were now fired on, and would not have escaped with their lives, had it not been for the proximity of the Treasury and the desire of the Sepoys for loot. And now those had to turn and flee who had passed an anxious day, collected within the narrow limits of the Flagstaff Tower, hoping against hope for a sign of dust on the Meerut Road, and surrounded by Sepoys, whose tempers could not be judged with accuracy.

And so let us leave Delhi for a while, in the hands of mutineers and of the scum of the population, looting on all sides, murdering all who called themselves Christians; cravens whom a few resolute men could keep at bay, while the odds were less than fifty to one. Over all was a pall of smoke from burning bungalows and from the stately mansion of Metcalfe House, which had been set on fire by the villagers of Chandrāwal.

It had, fortunately, been possible to send by telegraph to Umbālla some account of what had been happening at Delhi, and the general there was a man of action; he at once sent off his son to Simla with a copy of the telegram, for there was no wire to Simla in those days. It was not the centre of government, but merely a pleasant place to spend the summer in, should the governor-general or commander-in-chief so desire. The latter, General the Hon. George Anson, had been there for about a month, and had, on his way up, seen something of the trouble that was brewing. He was now to be very severely startled, although at first he did not seem to realize that any very serious defection had occurred. However, when he got a letter from Meerut, detailing the events there, he lost no time in ordering down to Umbālla three European regiments, cantoned at Dāgshāi, Subāthu, and Kasāuli, close to Simla. An officer was sent to arrange the preparation of a third-class siege-train at Phillour, and the Sirmur Gurkhas, who distinguished themselves so greatly, were ordered from Dehra Dun to Meerut. General Anson himself left for the plains on the morning of the 14th, to take command of the relieving force. The Maharāja of Patiāla sent troops to occupy Thanesar, and, later, Umbālla was confided to his care; the Maharāja of Jhind sent a contingent to Karnāl, and other chiefs assisted to guard the communications, for no reliance could now be placed on the Sepoy army.

The next few days were spent in the organization of transport by the civil authorities, in the supply to guns and infantry of ammunition, of which they had next to none, and in the collection of supplies of food and fodder. The troops were then pushed forward in small bodies to Karnāl, where General Anson died of cholera on the 27th of May. On that same evening a force at last left Meerut, and marched to Ghāzi-ud-din-nagar, now Ghaziābād, where, on the 30th of May and following day, it gave the rebels two sharp lessons, and repulsed their attacks with loss. On the 4th of June this force marched to effect a junction with the Umbālla force at Alipur, on the right bank of the Jumnā, and twelve miles from Delhi.

Sir Henry Barnard, on whom had devolved

the command, lost no time, after the arrival of the siege-train on the 6th, and of the Meerut force on the 7th, in advancing on Delhi. At 2 a.m. on the 8th of June the small army—seven hundred cavalry, two thousand five hundred infantry, and twenty-two guns—left camp, and at dawn came under the enemy's fire from their position at Badli-ki-Sarāi. The action was a short one, the guns were taken at the point of the bayonet by a dashing charge, and the cavalry, coming on the enemy's rear, completed the rout. Advancing still, in spite of wavering counsels, the general had the satisfaction of seeing the enemy brushed away and the Ridge retaken.

And now, so some contend, a still further advance might have seen the city taken, and the trials of a siege avoided. Certainly the maxim of *L'audace, toujours l'audace*, is one which both English and French have found most successful in engagements with Indian troops. But the men had already marched ten miles and had fought two actions; this, in the burning sun of the 8th of June, was enough for one day. Nor were the enemy disheartened or even content to allow them to rest. A heavy fire was opened from the walls, and an accurate one, for all the ranges had been previously tried, while in the afternoon the first of many attacks was delivered on the right of the position, so that the troops had to leave off pitching their camp to fight a third action. The rebels were repulsed, and night fell to the accompaniment of the boom of heavy guns, while our engineers were busily throwing up batteries for the guns and mortars, in order to reply to the cannonade. The day had diminished the small force by 184 casualties, to counterbalance which twenty-six guns had been captured, and a considerable number of the enemy killed or driven in panic to their homes.

But many mutineers had collected during the past month in Delhi, and on the 9th they again advanced to the attack of our right flank; they were again driven back, the Corps of Guides, which had arrived in the morning, after a march of five hundred and eighty miles in twenty-two days, lending valuable assistance. The 10th and 11th saw further attacks, and on the 12th of June the rebels surprised the left flank, and as nearly as possible got into camp. Fortunately help soon arrived, and the enemy were pursued with such vigour that Metcalfe House was occupied and henceforth held by piquets. The right was also attacked, but no ground was lost, and similar ill-success attended the efforts of the enemy on the 13th and 15th of June.

Meanwhile, the placing of guns in batteries at

Hindu Rāo's house, at the "Observatory," and on the General's Mound, steadily progressed, but they fired with little effect, while the heavier guns of the enemy battered Hindu Rāo's incessantly. A project to storm the city on the night of the 12th had been stopped by delay in withdrawal of the piquets, to the relief of all, except a few who were over-sanguine of success. An entrance might have been effected, but a disastrous expulsion would probably have followed.

On the 16th of June the rebels were reinforced by a body of mutineers from Nasirābād—certain prelude to a fresh attack, which was delivered on the 19th. Previously, on the 17th, an attack had been made from our side to stop the throwing up of a battery, which had been commenced in the Kishanganj sarāi, situated on the high ground just beyond the canal. The action was successful, and a source of possible annoyance stopped for the time being.

The attack of the 19th was a serious affair. The enemy this time kept away among the trees in the Sabzimandi, where they could only be observed with difficulty, suddenly appearing beyond the Ochterlony Garden in rear, and opening a hot fire. It was then nearly dusk, and the cavalry, hastily collected, were in some confusion; the troops had been under arms all day, uncertain when the attack might be delivered, and had just been dismissed to their tents. Consequently, for a time, the rebels had it all their own way, worked round astride of the line of communications, and nearly captured some of the guns; our gunners, in the darkness, fired on the cavalry, which was naturally very demoralizing. At last some infantry was sent out, and the enemy were slowly driven back until the firing gradually died out. At dawn the next morning there were no signs of the enemy, but they appeared later, only to hurry back to the city when our guns opened fire on them. This action cost us nearly a hundred casualties, and to prevent a repetition of a rear attack two heavy guns were put in a battery on the racecourse.

On the 21st of June the enemy received an additional reinforcement, in the shape of mutineers from Jullundur and Phillour, who marched across the bridge of boats unmolested by our guns, which could not range so far. Two days afterwards the first reinforcement from the Punjāb reached the camp, after making a double march, and only just in time. For June 23, 1857, was the centenary of Plassey, and saw another fierce attack from the Sabzimandi, the rebels fighting desperately, for they had been told that the day would see the end of British supremacy in India. It was a fearfully hot day; our men were quite exhausted by the sun's ardour, blinded by a terrible glare, and fainting for want of water. Three times were the gardens cleared of rebels, and not till sundown was the issue certain; but a substantial gain, to compensate for a hundred and sixty casualties, was the taking of a temple and sarai, in the Sabzimandi, which were later occupied by a piquet, and considerably protected this flank.

On the 27th of June the periodical rains set in, and the same day saw simultaneous attacks on the Metcalfe piquets, the Ridge batteries, and the Sabzimandi posts, but all were repulsed. A similar fate met an attack on the right, three days later. On the 28th of June and 1st and 2nd of July reinforcements reached the camp, but this accession of strength was more than counterbalanced by the arrival in the city of the Rohilkand brigade of mutineers, who crossed the river on the 1st of July, bands playing and colours flying, under the command of a subadar of artillery, Bakhtāwar Khān. The enemy's force was estimated to be fifteen thousand strong, while the besiegers did not muster more than five and a half thousand.

Great disappointment had been felt, and expressed, by the highest civil authorities that Delhi had not long ago been taken by storm; they rated the courage and fighting qualities of the mutineers at far too low a level; the experience of the troops, who were daily engaged with them, showed that they possessed a good deal of both. The civilian population were being plundered right and left, and therefore had no sympathy with the rebels; but they were completely cowed, and could be expected to give no aid to the avenging army. Still, the general felt that he might venture the "gambler's throw," and risk an assault, which he fixed for the dawn on the 3rd of July. On the 2nd it was found that treason was rife among some of the Hindustāni soldiers in camp, and such a number of them were felt to be untrustworthy, that it would have been unwise to leave them to guard the camp while the European soldiers were lost among the narrow lanes of Delhi. Moreover, the rebels had good information of the proposed attack, and moved out on the morning of the 3rd, after the orders for assault had been countermanded.

Later in the day the rebels devised the plan of cutting the communications by an attack on Alipur, and of capturing a convoy which was known by them to be on the road. They succeeded easily enough in attacking and capturing the village, but the convoy had been warned to halt; the mutineers had not the enterprise to go to meet it, or even to retain their position, but returned to Delhi on the following morning, meeting with some punishment on the way. Had there been a good general among the rebels in Delhi, and had he been allowed his way without interference, the result might have been very different indeed.

On the 5th of July Sir Henry Barnard died of cholera, the second commander of the Delhi field force to succumb to that dread disease. He was not in supreme command before Delhi, for General Anson had been succeeded, as provincial commander-in-chief, by Major-General T. Reed, C.B., H.M. Service, who, however, although he had arrived at Alipur on the night before the advance to Delhi, had left all arrangements, then and afterwards, in Sir H. Barnard's hands. He now assumed command of the field force, but the real commander was Colonel Neville Chamberlain, the adjutant-general.

On the 8th of July a series of operations for the destruction of the bridges over the canal and the Najafgarh drain was completed by the blowing up of the Bāssi bridge over the latter, some three miles distant from the camp. A strong escort of all arms accompanied the engineers, but did not see the enemy; while they were away a desperate attack was made on the Sabzimandi posts, which was repulsed with slight loss to us, but considerable slaughter among the enemy. Constant exertion on the part of the engineers had cleared away the houses and obstacles on this side, so that a clear field of fire was now obtainable.

On the 9th the irregular cavalry showed plainly that they were not to be trusted. Some of the 9th Irregular Cavalry were on patrol duty on the extreme right, and basely let in a body of rebel sowars, who suddenly charged the piquet near the General's Mound. A troop of the Carabineers broke at the unexpected charge, but the gallantry of a few officers, who dashed forward to a hand-to-hand engagement, and the steadfastness of the gunners, saved a disaster, and the invading sowars escaped with some difficulty and loss. Meanwhile, a furious cannonade was opened from the walls, and the enemy mustered thickly in the gardens towards the Sabzimandi, necessitating another "rat-hunt," at considerable loss to ourselves, for the list of casualties totalled 223. The irregular cavalry were now either sent away or disarmed, and the native horse artillery troop were deprived of their guns; several officers protested against this course, but Sir John Lawrence was peremptory about it, and there is no doubt that he was right.

All was now quiet until the 14th of July; possibly the enemy were sobered by recent heavy losses. But on that day they pluckily came on again, still on the Sabzimandi side; again there was a counter-attack on our part, utter contempt for the enemy leading our men to approach much too close to the walls, with the result that grape-shot caused a casualty roll of over two hundred, among whom was Colonel Neville Chamberlain, with his left arm splintered.

On the 16th there arrived the mutineers from Jhansi, and also intelligence of the assumption by Sir Patrick Grant, who had been summoned from Madras, of the office of commander-in-chief of the Bengal Army. So Major-General Reed, who was in very poor health, took sick leave, and handed over charge to Colonel Wilson, commandant of the Bengal Artillery, giving him the temporary rank of brigadier-general. This caused considerable annoyance to officers who were senior to Wilson, one or two of whom left the force. Exception also was taken to the appointment because he had been blamed to some extent for the indecision which had allowed the mutineers to escape unscathed from Meerut; but it was felt that he was the most efficient officer of senior rank for the post, and he gradually won the confidence of the men.

Major-General Reed left for the hills on the morning of the 17th, and an escort accompanied him as far as Alipur, guarding also a sick convoy which left at the same time. The presence of this escort prevented the carrying out of an attack on Alipur, which had been planned by the new arrivals from Jhansi; the idea was to draw off the troops in pursuit while other rebels attacked the camp, denuded of its defenders. The second part of the programme was carried out on the 18th, but the attack was again repulsed, and the enemy once more pursued; the officer commanding the counter-attack had, however, learnt experience, and would not allow the pursuit to be carried too far, while he conducted the retirement with great ability. He lost fewer men by far than was usual, yet the casualties amounted to over eighty. The enemy attacked again on the 20th and 21st, but neither side pressed hard. These constant affairs were realized to be expensive, and all idea of assault was definitely abandoned until after a preparation by siege-works.

On the 23rd the enemy brought guns out of the Cashmere Gate, and shelled the left of the position on the Ridge, our light guns replying, but with little effect. A small force was sent to stop the annoyance, and nearly took the guns, but failed owing to a misunderstanding and an unusual lack of dash. The next few days were very rainy, and all was quiet. On the 26th the rebels from Neemuch arrived, but they took some days' rest, and it was not until the 31st that a large force moved to the right rear of camp, with materials to repair one of the broken bridges over the drainage-cut, and thus get round in rear. The rain came down in torrents, but still they worked steadily on.

The 1st of August was the day of the "Bakra Id," one of the two great Mahomedan festivals. The enemy completed their bridge, and some had actually crossed, when a great flood came down the Najafgarh drain, as the result of the heavy rain of the day before and more rain on this day; the timbers of the bridge were carried away, so the rebels returned to the city. On their way a large force from the city met them, and the two bodies joining hurled themselves against the end of the Ridge. The attack commenced at sunset, and a heavy fire was kept up all night, fresh bodies renewing the attack as the defenders repulsed each effort. The shouting, bugling, and rattle of musketry were incessant all through the night and a great part of the following day, for it was not until about four o'clock in the afternoon that at length the rebels ceased their efforts. Now was seen the result of the constant work of the engineers to improve the trenches, for the casualties in this, the fiercest attack of all, did not amount to more than forty-six, of whom ten only were killed. The enemy naturally suffered heavily, a hundred and twenty-seven bodies being counted in one place alone.

This was enough to keep the enemy quiet for three days, but on the 6th of August they attacked the right batteries, once more without success. Under cover of this attack, and during the following night, they threw up a heavy-gun battery in Kishanganj; this opened fire on the 7th, and, after being silenced for a time, re-opened on the 8th, and kept up a most annoying fire, supplemented by rockets, which, however, were very erratic.

On the 7th the cartridge factory of the enemy was blown up, killing a considerable number, and causing much perturbation in the city. On this day also Brigadier John Nicholson came in by mail-cart, ahead of the Punjāb movable column which he commanded; he went round the position, and returned to his column on the 11th.

On the 8th the enemy, ever active, began shelling the Metcalfe piquets, and kept this up daily until it became unbearable. The general had promised Nicholson that his column should have the privilege of stopping this nuisance directly they arrived, but now decided not to wait. So, at dawn on the 12th, a small column surprised the sleeping rebels near Ludlow Castle, captured four guns and killed a number of them, but not without loss, for there were over a hundred casualties in this affair. The enemy were not a bit daunted, and started rocket-fire that evening, worrying the Metcalfe piquets with musketry all through the night, and finally ceased the annoyance at dawn on the 13th, after a week of constant firing. A week later they opened a heavy-gun battery across the river, which was clean out of range of any guns which were in position on that side; the fire of this battery made Coke's Rifles shift their camp, which was below the Flagstaff Tower on the city side of the Ridge.

On the 14th of August the column under Nicholson marched into camp to the music of the band of H.M. 8th Foot, and amid great enthusiasm. At midnight on the same day Hodson took a small party of horse and made a tour through the district around Rohtak, at which place he fought a brilliant little action with entire success; he returned on the 24th. On the night of the 19th Nicholson took out a small column to relieve Hodson's party, about the safety of which some nervousness was felt; but the road was impassable after heavy rain, and the troops soon returned, drenched through. Otherwise, nothing of importance happened before Delhi; bands played of an evening, and the rigours of campaigning were somewhat alleviated by the arrival of Parsee merchants with two thousand dozen of beer!

But this was only the lull before the storm, and the morning of the 24th saw the enemy come out in great force—some six thousand men with sixteen guns—and bear away to the south; they were evidently making a detour to cut the line of communications and intercept the siege-train. A strong column was at once ordered out, and Nicholson was given the command; they left at 4 a.m. on the 25th, marched by Azādpur, across the Pembāri Bridge over the canal, and made their way south-west by country roads. The rain came down in torrents, flooding the flat country and hollow roads, and making the ground so heavy that, after seven hours of marching, only nine miles had been covered. A halt was now called while a reconnaissance was made, which resulted in the discovery of the enemy some five miles further on, near the village of Najafgarh. The troops at once pressed forward, but a deep stream intervened, and it was not until about 5 p.m. that the column had crossed, the baggage having been left behind. Then events moved quickly. The key of the enemy's position was a walled garden on their left, so, while the right was held in check by some horse artillery guns, escorted by cavalry, the main body attacked the garden. Nicholson made a short speech, reminding the men of the battle of Chillianwallah, and how on that occasion fire was reserved until within short, charging distance, and he exhorted them to do the same. The guns poured in a rapid fire, the line advanced, poured in a volley at short range, and the garden was carried by storm in a few moments. Then the troops were reformed, the whole of the enemy's line was rolled up, thirteen guns were captured, and the rebels fled towards Delhi. Only part of the enemy's force was engaged, for the Rohilkand brigade had taken matters very leisurely, and were some distance behind, while the prompt attack did not admit of their coming up in time. The troops, hungry and tired, bivouacked on the field, and on the following morning, after breakfast, returned to camp, arriving there at dusk amid great enthusiasm.

Thus the last effort of the rebels was frustrated, and the Neemuch brigade of mutineers was practically destroyed, at a cost of a little over a hundred casualties. On the morning of the 26th the rebels came out from the city and attacked the camp, which they expected to find deserted, but soon discovered their mistake and retired. They made no further attack on our position until the siege-batteries were opened.

And now commenced the last chapter. All through the month of August the engineers had been busy, preparing gabions, fascines, and other materials in readiness to start the siege-works directly the train should arrive from Ferozepore. On the 27th of August a battery was commenced to the left of the "Sammy-house," to cover the construction of the real siege-batteries; the ground in front was cleared of brushwood, and survey operations were carried out. On the 4th of September in rumbled the siege-guns, drawn by elephants; they were at once altered for bullock draught, for elephants' will not take guns under fire, but the bullock is not sufficiently intelligent to mind. During the next few days came the last reinforcements, comprising, amongst others, the contingents of the Mahārājas of Jammu and Jhind. The effective strength was now about twelve thousand, but the contingents of the native states were very poorly armed indeed.

On the night of the 6th the "Sammy-house" battery was armed, and on the night of the 7th, while the guns on the Ridge opened fire to draw off the enemy's attention, the first siege-battery was traced, and constructed in two parts. There was little soil to be scraped on the spot, so sand-bags had been filled in readiness and kept close by; earth also was brought from the ravine and filled into gabions. Hundreds of camels were used to bring down the gabions and fascines of brushwood, and considering the confusion and the noise caused by these unwieldy animals, all mixed up in a mass with teams of bullocks bringing down the guns and cartloads of ammunition, it was marvellous that so much work was done that night, still more wonderful that the enemy did not hear the noise and open a devastating fire. However, they did not do more than send across a few rounds of grape until the morning, when they quickly awoke to the situation, and did not spare the scarcely completed and very partially armed batteries. During the night our men had been fortunate enough to be able to occupy the Kudsia Bāgh and Ludlow Castle without any opposition.

The morning of the 8th found the new

batteries receiving very warm attention from the Mori Bastion; but gradually the guns were got into position, and in the afternoon had almost silenced the guns on the bastion. The rebel gunners, however, who had fought splendidly all through, had not lost their pluck, and by various devices managed to keep up a slow fire. The left half of No. I. battery got to work on the Cashmere Gate; but this was only intended to be temporary, until the four guns could be moved into another and a closer battery. The enemy's cavalry made a sortie against the new batteries during the course of the day, but were met with showers of grape, and quickly retired with considerable loss. Nor did the enemy meet with any success when he opened fire, towards evening, with light guns and rockets from Kishanganj.

On the evening of the 8th the trees within the Kudsia Bāgh were cleared away, with the idea of establishing a battery there; but this was found impracticable. No. II. siege-battery was traced in two parts and commenced, but the experience of the previous night showed that the idea of making and arming a battery in one night was hardly practicable, so that things were taken more easily. No. II. battery was the big breaching battery of eighteen guns, on which all relied to do the bulk of the work;

it was to form the breach near the Cashmere Bastion.

On the night of the 9th was started the battery in the "Custom-house;" little could be done beyond sand-bagging, so as to obtain some shelter, and the working party was withdrawn at dawn. A battery for mortars was constructed on this same night under the cover afforded by some old buildings, which made a square, just outside the gate of the Kudsia Bāgh. This battery was armed, but did not open fire at once, for it was considered advisable for all to unmask together. The enemy were not idle, but kept up a continual fire, and made more than one sortie.

It was not until the morning of the 11th that the great breaching battery and the mortar battery opened fire, the men jumping on to the parapets, after the first salvo, and cheering lustily. The walls began at once to crumble under the heavy fire directed at such short range, and the shells knocked away the parapets in fine style. Yet the enemy were not disheartened, and pluckily started to mount guns elsewhere, while their cavalry had the audacity to attack the rear of the camp, but got severely punished.

The "Custom-house" battery did not open fire until the afternoon of the 12th, although it had been ready and armed on the previous night, but the embrasures required adjustment, which caused the delay. Some light mortars had been brought down to positions near by to lend their assistance, and to harass the enemy. And now the roar of fifty guns and mortars, great and small, filled the air. Some formed a breach in the curtain near the Water Bastion, others a breach near the Cashmere Bastion, others again, with the mortars, besides harassing the enemy with shells, tore away the musketry parapet all along the walls from the Water Bastion to beyond the Cashmere Gate, so that the stormers or the exploding party should not be exposed to the fire of men under cover. On the right the guns still pounded away at the Mori Bastion, and the enemy contributed their share to the din by constant fire from their enfilading battery outside the Cābul Gate, which did considerable execution as the shot crashed into our batteries from a flank.

For two days and two nights (during which salvos were fired every fifteen minutes) this went on, until our gunners and the cavalrymen who assisted them were nearly exhausted, for reliefs were not to be obtained. Come what might, the assault should not be delayed a day longer than could be helped, if the breaches were at all practicable; the engineers, after an examination on the night of the 13th, were able to report them to be so, although another twenty-four hours would make them still better. But this was quite enough, and the assault was ordered for the following morning.

Long before dawn the columns began to form up, each about a thousand strong: No. 1, under Nicholson, to storm the breach near the Cashmere Bastion, and to escalade the left face of the bastion; No. 2 to storm the Water Bastion breach, advancing from behind the "Custom-house" battery; No. 3 to advance down the road and enter the Cashmere Gate, after it had been blown in by the party under Home and Salkeld. Behind these three was a reserve column over twelve hundred strong, which the Rifles were to join after skirmishing in front of the storming columns. To the cavalry, about six hundred sabres, was given the task of guarding the batteries from a sortie, and away on the right the intrepid defender of Hindu Rāo's house, Major Reid, was to attack Kishanganj with No. 4 column—a scratch force drawn from the piquets and the Jammu contingent, which did not count for much, being badly disciplined and worse armed.

The main assault succeeded, although it had

to be made in broad daylight, for the guns had to reopen on the breaches, which had been repaired during the night. The Cashmere Gate was blown in, although the fire of the enemy nearly prevented the match being lighted, and killed more than one of the party; the walls were gained at the Cashmere and Water Bastions. But the enemy were not to be driven out of the city, and made just that stout resistance which had been anticipated by those who had demurred to the constant cry of "Why not assault?" in the early days of the siege. By evening hardly any of the city was held. On the left the Government College, Ahmad Ali Khān's house, and Skinner's house were occupied by the 3rd and Reserve Columns; but the rebels were still in the magazine, and had guns pointing down all the streets, along which further advance could not be made. The 3rd column had been nearly to the Jāma Masjid, but had been checked there; the rebels, coming down the Chāndni Chouk in great force, had almost cut them off, and had driven them back to the vicinity of Skinner's House. The 1st and 2nd columns had not been able to work round the walls beyond the Cābul Gate, in a narrow lane near which John Nicholson had fallen mortally wounded. The 4th column had completely failed, for the delay in the advance to the main assault had necessitated a wait, which had disclosed the intentions of this column to the enemy, who occupied Kishanganj, and gave them a very warm reception. Many of the men had found stores of liquor in the shops, had been unable to resist the temptation, and were in no condition for more fighting—were indeed hardly able to defend themselves. The total loss during the day had been 1170 officers and men killed and wounded. Had such a result followed an assault in the early days of the siege, it would have meant the withdrawal of the force, the spread of rebellion through the Punjāb, and the driving of the British into the sea.

The next five days saw continual fighting, each step forward being stubbornly contested. The heavy guns were brought into the city, and a bombardment started; the Magazine was taken at dawn on the 16th, and on the same morning the rebels evacuated Kishanganj, which was found to be very strongly fortified. On the 17th the Delhi Bank house was stormed. The posts were gradually pushed forward by sapping from house to house until nearly half the city was won, and the rebels and the population began to leave hurriedly. On the evening of the 19th the Burn Bastion was at last captured, after more than one failure; the following day saw the whole city and the palace in the hands of the exhausted troops. Headquarters were established in the Diwān Khās, and Major-General Wilson sent for a personal guard of the Sirmur Gurkhas, as a compliment to that gallant regiment. On the morning of the 21st a royal salute was fired to celebrate the victory.

On the morning of this same day Hodson, the "indefatigable," effected the capture of the King of Delhi, who had agreed to accompany the flying rebels, but had changed his mind and taken refuge at Humāyun's tomb. The place swarmed with armed men, but Hodson, with only fifty sowars, quietly insisted on the surrender, to which the king agreed, on condition that his life should be spared; he was lodged in the palace without mishap, to the surprise of the general, who had sanctioned the enterprise, but did not expect its success. On the following day Hodson again proceeded to the tomb and effected the capture of three princes of the royal house—Mirzā Moghal, Mirzā Khizr Sultān, and Mirzā Abu Bakr. He sent them off under escort, and remained himself to disarm their followers; having done so, he galloped after them, and found the escort threatened by a crowd. No promise of life had been extended to the princes, and Hodson deemed a rescue possible, so he shot them himself—a regrettable action perhaps, but one which cannot dim the lustre of his memory as a brave soldier.

On the 23rd of September John Nicholson, that lion-hearted hero, died at the early age of thirty-five, after suffering agony for nine days, but bearing it with extraordinary fortitude. He was buried on the following day in the Cashmere Gate Cemetery, just outside the walls which he had been the first to mount. On the same day a force left Delhi to relieve Agra, and to bear an honourable part in the Relief of Lucknow, thereby adding fresh laurels to those so gallantly earned before Delhi.

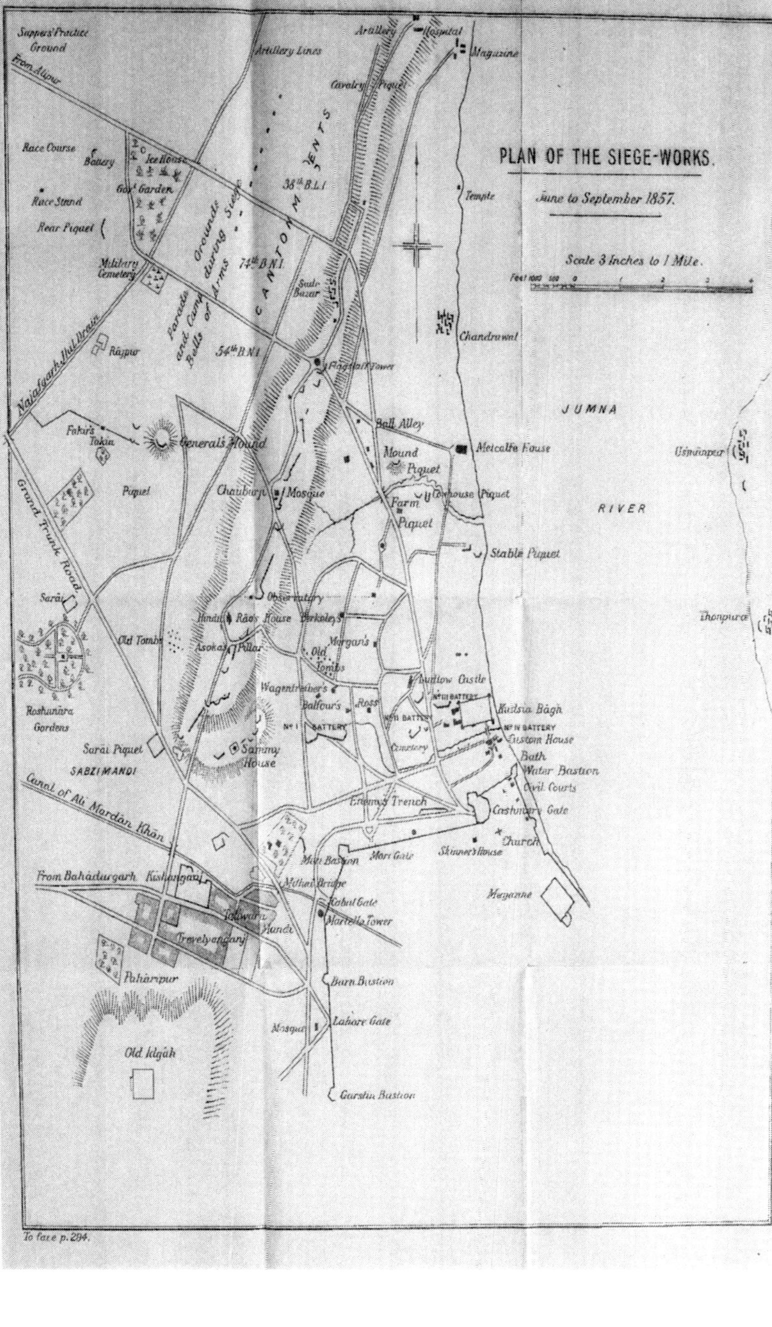
PLAN OF THE SIEGE-WORKS.
June to September 1857.
Scale 3 Inches to 1 Mile.
Sappers' Practice Ground
From Alipur
Artillery Lines
Artillery
Hospital
Magazine
Cavalry Piquet
Race Course
Battery
Ice House
Gov! Garden
Race Stand
Rear Piquet
CANTONMENTS
38th B.L.I.
74th B.N.I.
54th B.N.I.
Parade and Camping Grounds during Siege
Bells of Arms
Temple
Military Cemetery
Sadr Bazar
Chandrawal
Najafgarh Jhil Drain
Rajpur
Flagstaff Tower
JUMNA
RIVER
Fakir's Takia
General's Mound
Metcalfe House
Mound Piquet
Usmanpur
Piquet
Chauburji Mosque
Cowhouse Piquet
Farm Piquet
Stable Piquet
Grand Trunk Road
Sarai
Observatory
Hindu Rao's House
Berkeley's
Thonpura
Old Tombs
Asoka's Pillar
Morgan's
Old Tombs
Wagentreiber's
Ludlow Castle
Balfour's
Ross
No III BATTERY
Kudsia Bagh
No I BATTERY
No II BATTERY
No IV BATTERY
Roshanara Gardens
Custom House
Sarai Piquet
Sammy House
Cemetery
Bath
Water Bastion
SABZIMANDI
Civil Courts
Canal of Ali Mardan Khan
Enemy's Trench
Cashmere Gate
Church
Mori Bastion
Mori Gate
Skinner's House
From Bahadurgarh
Kishanganj
Mithai Bridge
Magazine
Kabul Gate
Martello Tower
Teliwara
Mandi
Trevelyanganj
Paharipur
Burn Bastion
Mosque
Lahore Gate
Old Idgah
Garstin Bastion

To face p. 294.

CHAPTER XII

DELHI SINCE 1857

The city under a military governor—Advance of the Jodhpur Legion—Battle of Narnoul—Trial of prominent rebels and of the king—Delhi transferred to the Punjab—Assumption of government by the Crown—Proclamation of a British Empress of India—Delhi the commercial capital of Northern India.

THE recaptured city was put under martial law, a military governor was appointed, and search was made through all the wards for any Sepoys who might be lurking there in disguise; numbers of them were captured and executed, hundreds of others, after a while, when the fierce desire for vengeance had somewhat abated, were sent for transportation to the Andaman Islands. But the gallows erected in the Chāndni Chouk took a heavy toll; as the natives said, "Your vengeance is not dealt out in a day, like that of our previous conquerors." In this they were hardly historically correct; but what they meant was that Timur and Nādir Shāh massacred and were done with it, while no man who had been connected with the Mutiny could ever feel safe, even years after. There was also a strict search made for loot of all kinds, which had been promised by Major-General Wilson to the soldiers; but Lord Canning took the view that all loot, the ownership of which could not be identified, was the property of Government, promise or no promise. As some compensation for the trials and dangers of a long siege, he awarded the soldiers six months' "batta," or field allowances, amounting to the paltry sum of thirty-eight rupees. One of the wounded soldiers, several of whom had lost a limb in the assault, chalked on the wall of the hospital in Delhi, "Delhi taken, and India saved, for thirty-eight rupees, or one rupee, eleven annas, eight pies a battle!" The board of directors of the East India Company were pleased to ratify Lord Canning's action, but doubled the amount of the "batta," and this was all that the war-worn veterans got beyond the gratitude of their countrymen.

The native inhabitants of the city were all turned out owing to the murders of certain European soldiers, and for some time only Hindus were allowed to return. It was a moot point, indeed, whether the whole city (or at least the Jāma Masjid and the palace) should not be razed to the ground; but such counsels could hardly be seriously entertained. The city was garrisoned by that portion of the Delhi field force which had not been sent to relieve Agra and Lucknow, and the tired soldiers had a good rest, but there was still work for them to do.

At the beginning of November intelligence was received of the approach of the Jodhpur Legion, which had mutinied at Erinpura and Mount Abu; a small force was sent, on the 10th of November, towards Rewāri to engage the rebels, some two thousand strong. The going was very heavy, and the big guns sank to their axles while crossing the sandy beds of the rivers, so that it required the united strength of five elephants to pull them through. On the 16th the column was able to engage the enemy at Narnoul in a completely successful action, killing about a hundred and fifty of them. The column then returned to Delhi. Other small forces also were sent from time to time to search the country, and to destroy wandering bands of mutineers; eventually the troops in garrison were quartered in the Government College and the house of Ahmad Ali Khān, Skinner's house being the officers' mess. In 1859 the native infantry were cantoned in Dariāganj, and barracks were built in the palace for a wing of European infantry and a company of artillery; many buildings outside within a range of five hundred yards were swept away, and the palace has always since then been known as the Fort.

We have slightly anticipated a number of important events which had occurred meanwhile. Towards the end of the year 1857 the principal accessories to the Mutiny were indicted before military commissions. On the 13th of October two more sons of the old king, Mirzā Bakhtāwar Shāh and Mirzā Mahndu, having been found guilty, were shot in the Jumna river-bed by a party of riflemen. Then followed the trials of Nahar Singh, Rāja of Ballabgarh, and Nawāb Abdul Rahmān Khān of Jhajjar, against whom the principal witness was Sir John Theophilus Metcalfe. The father of the former chief had been granted the lands surrounding Ballabgarh, a few miles south of Delhi, by General Lord Lake, in 1803, on condition that he should adequately police the Muttra Road as far as Palwal. In those days dense jungle bordered the road on either side, while thieves, dacoits, and Thugs carried on their nefarious trade unmolested. Now the opening of the Agra Canal has caused the forest to disappear, and crops have taken its place. Both these chiefs were found guilty, their lands were confiscated by Government, and they themselves were hanged in the Chāndni Chouk about the end of the year.

On January 27, 1858, the old king himself was brought to trial before a military commission, composed of three "Queen's" and two "Company's" officers, on four charges, including the murder of forty-nine persons within the palace on the 16th of May. The trial lasted twenty-one days; a great many witnesses were called, including his own physician, Ahsanulla Khān; a quantity of documentary evidence was read, and all proved that he had given in his lot with the mutineers, and had assumed (as well as he could) the functions of royalty. That other and more astute minds had stirred up the Sepoys to mutiny seems almost certain; but he and his sons had definitely cast in their lot with them. The king had actually been one of the first to inform the Lieut.-Governor at Agra of the outbreak, but had afterwards gone with the tide which indeed he could never have stemmed. He was found guilty of every one of the charges; but there was no desire to visit on him the extreme penalty, even had not promise of his life been extended to him. He was deported to Rangoon with his favourite queen, Zinat Mahal, and their son, Jiwan Bakht, and there he died in 1862.

On January 11, 1858, Delhi was made over

to the civil authorities, and the civil courts were reopened in the following July. Most of the records had been destroyed during the troubles. On February 6, 1858, the Delhi territory was transferred from the jurisdiction of the North-West Provinces to the Punjāb, as by right of conquest, and the Hissār and Delhi districts were formed.

On November 1, 1858, the Crown assumed the government of India by the proclamation which has become so famous. The governor-general was now termed Viceroy, and the Company's army was absorbed into the royal army. This took a little time to accomplish, and a certain amount of trouble was experienced, the European soldiers refusing to transfer their services without a bounty; there was what was called "The White Mutiny." It is possible that the niggardly treatment after the Siege of Delhi had something to do with this; but many took their discharge rather than join the forces of the Crown. Eventually, in 1861, matters were satisfactorily settled, a bounty was given, and those who transferred their services were permitted to count their previous service for pension.

The Company's European Regiments were numbered from 101 to 109, the First European Bengal Fusiliers becoming the 101st Foot; in

1868 they went to England for the first time as a Regiment.

About the year 1870 the Mutiny Memorial on the Ridge was erected, to the memory of the officers and men who had died during the siege, by their comrades. In 1865 Dr. Cotton, Bishop of Calcutta, laid the foundation-stone of St. Stephen's Church, near the Queen's Gardens, as a memorial to the martyred Christians who fell at Delhi. The church was opened on May 10, 1867, the tenth anniversary of the massacre. There had been a Delhi Mission for some years previously to 1857, started by voluntary contributions from those who attended St. James's Church. The Society for the Propagation of the Gospel had lent its aid since 1854, and one of the missionaries, the Rev. A. R. Hubbard, was among the victims. After the Mutiny year the mission was re-established, and in 1877 the Cambridge University Mission was amalgamated with it. The efforts of the mission in the direction of education have been great, much good has been done by the establishment of hospitals, but the progress of conversion has been very slow in the barren soil of Delhi. There has also been a Baptist Mission since 1813, and the Rev. J. Mackay took a noble part as a non-combatant in the defence of the house in

Dariāganj; he was taken prisoner there and murdered.

The population of Delhi in 1847 numbered about a hundred and sixty thousand, but the Mutiny of 1857 caused a diminution in that number of over twenty thousand; so gradually did they return that in 1875 the inhabitants numbered only as many as in 1847. In the last thirty years, however, nearly fifty thousand additional people have crowded in, and Delhi has become the commercial capital and distributing centre for the whole of the northern portion of India. This is due to the fact, of which the old founder could never have dreamt, that Calcutta, Bombay, and Karachi are almost equi-distant.

In 1857 the East Indian Railway had been opened from Calcutta to Rāniganj, a distance of a hundred and twenty miles only; but the work of construction was in active progress up to Delhi. The alignment chosen from Agra was to the west of the Jumna, and a portion of the bank then thrown up may still be traced. After the Mutiny the railway was taken from Tundla Junction, *viâ* Aligarh, to the east bank of the Jumna at Chola; this section was opened in 1864. The bridge was then still under construction, and the first regular train did not run into Delhi until January 1, 1867; the bridge, it may be mentioned, is over half a mile in length. In the same year the Sind, Punjāb, and Delhi Railway entered by means of running powers granted from Ghaziābād Junction.

In 1873 the Rājputana State Railway connected Delhi with Bombay, and in 1891 the Delhi-Umballa-Kalka Railway gave a shorter route to the north. In 1897 the Southern Punjāb Railway was opened to traffic, and afforded a much shorter route to Karachi. In 1900 the opening of the Ghaziābād-Moradābād Railway, and the granting of running powers, gave the Oudh and Rohilkand Railway an entrance from the east, and a shorter broad-gauge link with Bombay was given when the Agra-Delhi Chord Railway was opened on March 1, 1905, on much the same route as that originally proposed for the East Indian Railway.

Thus seven lines of railway radiate from Delhi which has regained much of its former importance.

In 1876 the present Emperor (then Prince of Wales) visited Delhi, and the regiments which had garrisoned the Main piquet in Hindu Rao's house took up their old positions on the Ridge. He was also entertained at a ball in the Diwān Khās, where the health of Queen Victoria had been proposed and drunk with acclamation after the recapture of the city. On the 1st of January in the following year the first British Empress of India was proclaimed, according to ancient custom, at Delhi; the present emperor also was proclaimed there on January 1, 1903. The many camps round Delhi, the long procession of elephants, the presence of Mahomedan and Hindu feudatories from all India—all combined to recall the splendour, which Delhi has known in the past, which we have traced in the history of the Seven Cities.

APPENDIX

LIST OF WORKS CONSULTED

Archæology

1. *Āsār-us-sanādid (Urdu).* By Sāyyad Ahmad Khān. 1847.
2. *Description des Monuments de Delhi en 1852, d'apres le texte Hindustani de Saiyid Ahmad Khan.* By M. Garcin de Tassy. 1861.
3. *Journal of the Archæological Society of Delhi,* 1850.
4. *Essays on Indian Antiquities.* By James Prinsep, F.R.S. Edited by Edward Thomas, F.R.S. 1858.
5. *Asiatic Researches.*
6. *The Ancient Geography of India.* By Sir Alexander Cunningham, K.C.I.E. 1871.
7. *Archæological Survey of India, Reports.* By the same Author and others. 1862, &c.
8. *Archæology of Delhi.* By Carr Stephen. 1876.
9. *Journal of a Route across India, &c.* By Lieut.-Col. Fitz-Clarence. 1819.
10. *Handbook for Visitors to Delhi.* By H. G. Keene, M.R.A.S. 1899.
11. *Delhi, Past and Present.* By H. C. Fanshawe, C.S.I. 1902.
12. *Journal of the Royal Asiatic Society.*
13. *Selections from the Journal of the Bengal Asiatic Society.*

History

14. *Brief History of the Indian People.* By Sir W. W. Hunter.
15. *Ancient India; its invasion by Alexander the Great.* By J. W. McCrindle. 1896.

16. *History of Hindustan.* By Mahomed Kasim Ferishta, of Delhi. Translated by Alexander Dow. 1768.
17. *Mahomedan History.* By Major David Price. 1811.
18. *Chronicles of the Pathan Kings of Delhi.* By Edward Thomas, F.R.S. 1871; with supplement, 1896.
19. *Travels of Ibn Batuta.* Translated by the Rev. Samuel Lee. 1829.
20. *Life of Babar, including his Memoirs.* By R. M. Caldecott. 1844.
21. *A History of India under Babar and Humayun.* By W. Erskine. 1854.
22. *Ain-i-Akbari of Abul Fazl.* Translated by H. Blochmann. 1873.
23. *Memoirs of the Emperor Jahangir.* Translated by Major David Price. 1829.
24. *Hakluytus Posthumus, or Purchas, his Pilgrimes.* 1625.
25. *Travels in the Moghal Empire* (1656–1668). By François Bernier. Edited by Archibald Constable. 1891.
26. *Travels in India.* By Jean Baptiste Tavernier. Edited by V. Ball, LL.D., &c. 1889.
27. *The Moghul Empire.* By H. G. Keene. 1866.
28. *History of Nadir Shah.* By James Fraser. 1742.
29. *Military Memoirs of George Thomas.* By Capt. W. Francklin. 1803.
30. *Memoir of the War in India, &c.* By Major William Thorn. 1818.
31. *Notes on the Siege of Delhi* (1804). By Major-General Galloway, C.B.
32. *Scenes in Hindustan.* By Emma Roberts. 1835.
33. *Rambles and Recollections of an Indian Official.* By Major-General W. H. Sleeman. 1844.
34. *Travels in India.* By Capt. Leopold von Orlich 1845.
35. *Narrative of a Journey, &c.* By the Right Rev. Reginald Heber, D.D., Bishop of Calcutta. 1849.

Appendix

MISCELLANEOUS

36. *East India Register.*
37. *Indian Postal Guide.*
38. *Delhi Gazetteer.*
39. *River Training and Control on the Guide Bank System.* By F. J. E. Spring, C.I.E. (Technical Section Papers in the Public Works Department).
40. *Dictionary of Islam.* By Hughes. 1896.

VIEWS, ETC.

41. *Oriental Scenery.* By Thomas and William Daniell. 1816.
42. *Ruins of Gaur.* By H. Creighton, 1817.
43. *Photographs of Delhi, Agra, and Rajputana.* By Impey. 1865.

The works consulted for the chapter on the "Siege of Delhi" are too numerous to mention here.

INDEX

Index

Index

Index

Index

Index

Index

Index

Index

Index

Index

THE END